Psychological Consulting to Management

A Clinician's Perspective

PSYCHOLOGICAL CONSULTING TO MANAGEMENT

A Clinician's Perspective

Lester L. Tobias, Ph.D.

BRUNNER/MAZEL, *Publishers* • New York

Library of Congress Cataloging-in-Publication Data

Tobias, Lester L.

    Psychological consulting to management : a clinician's perspective
    Lester L. Tobias.
      p. cm.
    Includes bibliographical references.
    ISBN 0-87630-564-8
    1. Psychology, Industrial.   2. Management—Psychological aspects.
   3. Clinical psychology.   I. Title.
    [DNLM: 1. Administrative Personnel—psychology.   2. Psychology,
   Clinical.   3. Psychology, Industrial.   HF5548.8 T629p]
   HF5548.8.T57   1989
   658'.001'9—dc20
   DNLM/DLC
   for Library of Congress   89-22098
                                                           CIP

Published by
BRUNNER/MAZEL, INC.
19 Union Square
New York, New York 10003

Manufactured in the United States of America

10 9 8 7 6 5 4 3 2 1

For
Andrea,
and for
Julia and Lauren,
whose daddy helps people
who tell him secrets

Contents

Acknowledgments

I wish to thank Ed Glazer for allowing me to incorporate some of his unpublished material into this book. Tom Sutherland provided valuable insights and editorial comments on the manuscript. Peter Gilbert, Ed Keyes, and the late Woody Senderling have all stimulated my thinking, as have other members of the National Psychological Consultants to Management. My former partner, Dan Tear, taught me more about consulting psychology than anyone, and I am in his debt. My wife, Andrea F. Tobias, provided helpful cultural and linguistic perspectives. Barbara Sonnenschein, the late Ann Alhadeff, Natalie Gilman, and Laura Greeney of Brunner/Mazel provided me valuable direction and feedback during the writing of this book.

I am most deeply grateful to my mentors-colleagues-partners at Nordli, Wilson Associates for their continuing friendship, stimulation, encouragement, and shared commitment to ideals, as well as for their support for this project. Larry Foley, Paul Harpin, and Rudy Lessing provided helpful anecdotes. Jim Dowding, Tony Saccone, and especially Jim Abrams were of immense help with feedback and editorial comments. I am particularly indebted to John Clizbe, not only for his painstaking criticism and incisive wisdom throughout this project but, more important, for his persistent faith and encouragement.

I want to thank Penny Peloquin and Eileen Gabis and Maria Litynsky for their conscientious assistance with the many secretarial and word-processing tasks this book required. Janet Lee, Marie Mersereau, and Ellie Walinsky were each very helpful in proofing and in providing back-up support.

Last, I owe a debt to countless clients for their enrichment and for teaching me more than they knew they had about human potentials.

•　•　•

I write this book in respectful memory of Bill Nordli and Watson Wilson, not only for what they gave me personally, but for the tradition of wisdom and humanity they handed on.

Lester L. Tobias
Westborough, Massachusetts

Prologue

I discovered management psychology while looking for a clinical job at a convention. I had worked in a variety of clinical settings and was looking for greater challenge and fulfillment. The man I met at the convention told me little about what he actually did as a management psychologist, but a lot about how he felt about what he did. He said that he loved working with bright and successful executives who are highly motivated to improve themselves. He enjoyed being able to indirectly influence the lives of many people by working with their bosses and helping to improve an organization's culture. He relished the diversity of personal challenges that he faced and the excitement of the business challenges his client companies faced. He also thrived on the accountability to which his clients held him—for wise counsel, for cultural impact, and for predictions that had to come true. He liked being *on the line* and he liked feeling that he was making a significant difference. There was an energy in what he said that I had been looking for in my own career—and had not yet found—and I pretty much knew then what I wanted to do.

I have not been disappointed. For me it has turned out to be what it was cracked up to be, and I think that it has turned out that way for others too. A while back, I did a study with 25 members of the National Psychological Consultants to Management. They had a median of 28 years of consulting experience. They were asked to compare their overall job satisfaction with that of the executives with whom they work, and 18 of 25 responded that their rate was "well above average," with five reporting "above average," and the remaining two reporting "average" satisfaction. Apparently, I am not alone.

In 1985, I attended the "Evolution of Psychotherapy" convention in Phoenix, Arizona, which included among its speakers many of the most eminent psychotherapists of the twentieth century (Zeig, 1988). I was struck by how much of what these speakers presented was *old stuff,* by how much of what they presented was simply the common language of the psychology with which I grew up professionally. At the same time, I realized that it was these people whose original contributions made up what was now *old stuff.* Perhaps, a mark of a good idea is that it becomes so commonplace that its originator is forgotten. My own influences have been so diverse that I hope my failure to reference the originators of the ideas in this book is seen as a similar compliment, and not as disrespect. The reader should not assume that any of the ideas in this book are original.

This book is written in an attempt to provide clinicians with some intellectual extensions for conceptualizing the psychological consulting process. It is hoped that it will also help stimulate non-clinically-trained consultants to consider the clinician's viewpoint in order to deepen their perspectives and to more completely account for the variance they see in their consulting work. I will try to show how the clinical frame of mind naturally applies in the organizational context. I will portray consulting as a process, just as psychotherapy is a process, and I will emphasize perspectives rather than techniques.

This is not a book about psychotherapy, behavior change, social change, personality theory, clinical assessment, or other relevant areas of scholarly or clinical endeavor. I assume the reader is already well-versed in a number of these areas and knowledgeable enough to fill in the gaps when necessary. Nor is it my intent to systematically cover, compare, or contrast the many other approaches to consulting or insights about change that round out and enrich the particular perspective of this book. Instead, I wish to provide a sense of a process, a feel for the issues, and a degree of linkage between the readers' experience and my own. Further, the book does not attempt to deal with the issue of *how* one maintains objectivity or how one deals with resistance, transference, or value conflicts; rather, it tries to show *where* objectivity may tend to be challenged, where change tends to be blocked, and where value conflicts tend to occur in the organizational consulting context. I assume, then, that the reader has already developed a personal style that incorporates self-scrutiny, where values come into play within a conscious framework and as part of a therapeutic strategy. This book, then, is about, and is an attempt at, empowerment.

Humanizing the workplace is one of the great challenges of an economic system. Humanizing implies two things to me: Caring about people and being realistic about people. Caring alone can do little unless the energy of caring is expressed with an understanding of psychological reality. Conversely, the ability to care is dissipated by perceptual distortion, ignorance of psychological causality, and feelings of incapacity. Organizations flourish as the individuals who comprise them grow and maximize their potentials. It is the consultant's job to help foster this symbiosis. To my mind, a central commitment of the management psychologist is to help managers confront psychological realities, so they may more easily allow themselves to care.

Psychological Consulting to Management

A Clinician's Perspective

1

What Is Psychological Consulting to Management?

We never know how high we are
Till we are called to rise;
And then, if we are true to plan,
Our statures touch the skies.

Emily Dickinson ("Aspiration")

Consulting psychology, management psychology, or corporate psychology, as it is variously called, is the application of the principles of psychology to help people in organizations become more effective (DuBrin, 1982). Its history has cut across and borrowed from the specialities of clinical and counseling psychology[1], guidance counseling[2], personnel psychology[3], sociology[4], personality and social psychology[5], and industrial and organizational psychology[6], and it shares with all of psychology a century of research, theory, methodology, and applied wisdom (also, see Mangham, 1978, for contrasts between "systems," "humanism," and "interactionists"). Its practitioners tend to hail from the applied disciplines, and each imparts to the interdisciplinary soup the flavors of that individual's specialty cuisine and theoretical tastes.

The origins of management psychology are, therefore, wide-ranging. Many of its roots are undocumented, since the field was invented many times and in many different ways by individual practitioners, who primarily passed along their knowledge orally, if at all, and usually only to close colleagues or members of their firms.

1

Two broad traditions can be distilled, roughly corresponding to the industrial and organizational specialty and the clinical and counseling specialty. The former emphasized the study of groups, social processes and social structures and, typically, employed large-scale assessment strategies; the latter focused more on individuals, personality theory, and the assessment of individuals. Each tradition tended to define organizational processes and problems within its own semantic, linguistic, and theoretical framework and measured them with its own measuremental research methodology and technology. The practitioners of the industrial and organizational tradition found problems of morale, or productivity, or organizational structure. The clinicians found executives not working up to their potentials, leaders reenacting their family dramas, and workers whose strengths and weaknesses were misaligned with their assigned tasks.

In designing interventions, each tradition focused most on those independent variables that were the stock-and-trade of their specialties. Those who studied organizations modified environmental variables and worked with groups, whereas those more clinically inclined focused on changing individuals through one-on-one interventions. A practical, real-world basis was added by the personnel psychologists, who had been focusing on predicting sales performance, designing and evaluating training programs, and measuring performance and morale.

In the course of consulting, the organizational psychologists were impressed by the degree of impact single individuals could have—both positively and negatively—in setting the tone, in bringing out the best and worst in others, and in promoting or blocking change. They began to notice how these individuals' personalities and developmental histories predisposed them, sometimes automatically, toward certain actions. The clinicians, on the other hand, were increasingly impressed by the power of organizations to elicit the talents and flaws in individuals—how what was maladaptive at an organizational level could be adaptive at an individual level, how thwarted individual strengths could become organizational liabilities, how organizational cultures facing the age-old dilemmas of liberty versus order played the music which individuals danced. As perspectives widened, the traditions borrowed from each other, consciously as well as unconsciously, and many cross-specialty wheels were reinvented in the process since it was the perspectives that changed rather than the nature of people in organizations.

Management psychologists, then, are people who look at organizations from one or more of a number of psychological perspectives. They explore organizational problems and opportunities and look at groups of people and at individuals using psychological methods. They apply psychological principles in order to help the people in organizations to be more effective.

The issues management psychologists address include:

- Strengthening employee morale

- Upgrading hiring practices

- Improving organizational cultures

- Helping individuals reach their potentials

- Promoting teamwork

- Enhancing communication

- Maximizing the good fit between a person and a job

- Helping people and organizations cope with stress

- Reducing unhealthy organizational conflicts

- Reducing employee turnover

- Fostering creativity and broader, deeper, and more objective thinking

- Implementing programs which can succeed because they better account for human nature

- Helping organizations encourage, assess, and reward individual and group goal attainment

- Helping people or groups in crisis to cope

- Helping fired employees move on with their lives

- Helping managers to help their people develop and grow while contributing to organizational objectives.

In short, they may well deal with anything and everything that has impact on the growth and satisfaction of people in organizations.

Management psychologists deal with people one-on-one, in groups, and in seminars and classrooms. They work at client companies and at their own offices. Their written work ranges from psychological evaluations of executives to reports of the results of attitude surveys. The consulting psychologist serves as a sounding board, an objective outsider with no ax to grind, who usually promises confidentiality. The psychologist helps develop psychological job descriptions, interviews job applicants, provides them with feedback once they are hired, and helps them and their managers cope with each other more effectively as time goes on. The psychologist may serve as a clinician, a counselor, an assessor, a teacher, and an expert in psychological techniques and perspectives.

The tools of the psychological consultant in industry include tests of intelligence, personality, motivation, cognitive style, managerial style, interests, and aptitudes. Many provide or use various appraisal forms, self-development guides, attitude surveys, peer feedback forms, performance review forms, as well as many others. Some forms measure individuals and groups of individuals; some measure progress; and others are meant to stimulate. Some psychologists may do formal validations or other forms of research, although most focus primarily upon applications. Given this wide-ranging laundry list, some mention of what management psychology is *not* is in order. It is not human engineering or consumer psychology, at least as it is most widely practiced. The practitioner may well, however, borrow from these fields. Similarly, the provision of employee assistance programs[7] or other variants of on- or off-location delivery of psychotherapy would not usually be a defining characteristic of psychological consulting to management, although management psychologists may well offer these types of services.

A CLINICAL APPROACH

There are many valid ways to consult to management, and the valid ways have much in common. Therefore, the clinical approach to management psychology is defined by its relative position on various continua and by what is emphasized or not emphasized, rather than by adherence to any particular dogma.

The clinical approach shares with other psychological approaches a deep appreciation for the complexities of psychological causality and for the wealth of research supporting it. It appreciates the embeddedness of the individual within his or her social and cultural context. It tends, however, to stress intrapsychic causation and idiographic variables more, and it tends to focus on individuals in addressing the problems of social systems. Its emphasis is on how the growth of individuals facilitates organizational change, rather than *vice versa*.

Although the clinical approach, like other psychological approaches, recognizes the myriad ways in which human beings interpret, redefine, and distort reality, it tends to place greater emphasis than other approaches on defensive barriers and personality factors as they play themselves out within a situational or interpersonal context.

In addition, the clinical approach shares with others a recognition of the fallibility of the change agent, of how bounded we are by our own cultural and defensive biases, by our own maturity, and by our stage in the life-cycle. However, the clinical approach tends to place greater emphasis on consistent inner scrutiny by the consultant in the never-ending struggle to maintain objectivity and to distinguish between the realities of the client-clinician relationship and the client's "real" life, as well as between the therapist's perceptions and subjective experience and those of the client.

Clinicians tend to emphasize going deeper and deeper, reading into and reading beyond, and they reflexively seek out "more than meets the eye." They are constantly questioning their own role, their own impact, their own hidden agendae, and their own inner motivation. They see themselves as simultaneously part and not part of the system, and they constantly strive to maintain a healthy equilibrium between these two roles. They strive to understand boundaries.

Clinicians tend to be patient. They recognize that the way people view, experience, and approach their world is rooted in their developmental histories and, therefore, that growth may require some time for unraveling. Clinicians tend to recognize that people's readiness to grow is often unpredictable and transitory and, therefore, that the clinician must have a good sense of timing and adopt flexible and opportunistic strategies in order to know when to plant and when to harvest.

They see themselves as catalysts, as enablers who help people unshackle themselves from static predispositions. They do not overcommit their expectations to a predetermined result, trusting instead in the *process* of freeing up each individual's unique ability and readiness to explore alternatives. They constantly look for answers in the restatement and redefinition of problems and, especially as they gain maturity and experience, they increasingly become acutely aware of the difference between being expert and being helpful.

Finally (and perhaps most controversially), clinicians are inclined to define the client as the individual more than the organization. They work from the fundamental premise that the organization will reap rewards because the individual grows. The organization (which typically pays the bill) benefits *because* the individual is the client. It is not a matter of "either/or" loyalty on the part of the clinician; it is a matter of focus and priority.

None of these emphases are the distinct province of clinicians, but they are characteristic of the clinician's focus and of the training and supervisory traditions that start them on their ways. These emphases form the basis of the language in which clinicians communicate with one another and the common assumptions that they share. While we all recognize that individual perspective and practice vary considerably among those trained in the clinical perspective as well as those trained in other fields of psychology, this basic approach, in my opinion, is one which would serve the consulting psychologist well in his relationship with the client company.

1. See Flory, 1965; French, Caplan & Van Harrison, 1982; Glaser, 1958; Grant, Katkovsky, & Bray, 1967; Haire, 1959; Jennings, 1967; Kahn, 1980; Kornhauser, 1965; Langer, 1969; Leavy & Freedman, 1956; Levinson, 1962, 1964, 1972; Levinson et al., 1962; Manuso, 1983; McLean, 1958; McMurray, 1959; Menninger & Levinson, 1954; Muench, 1960; Ohmann, 1957; Sadler, 1960.

2. See Brown, Brooks & Assoc., 1984; Gutteridge, 1980; Hackman & Oldham, 1980; Herr & Cramer, 1979; Holland, 1985; Holland, Magoon & Spokane, 1981; Kotter, Faux & McArthur, 1978; Krumbholtz & Hamel, 1982; Montross & Shinkman, 1981; Morgan, 1980; Osipow, 1983; Schein, 1978; Souerwine, 1978; Tolbert, 1980; Walker & Gutteridge, 1979; Whiteley & Resnikoff, 1978.

3. See Bellows, 1961; Campbell et al., 1970; Gould, 1970; Miner, 1969.

4. See Buckley, 1967, 1968; Kohn & Schooler, 1983; Miller, 1951.

5. See Allport, 1931, 1960; Fiske & Taylor, 1984; Katz & Kahn, 1966; Magnusson & Endler, 1977; Schneider, 1973; Snyder & Icker, 1985; Weick, 1979; Wiggins, 1973.

6. See Argyris, 1985; Bass, 1965; Beckhard & Harris, 1987; Bennis & Nanus, 1985; Bennis et al., 1975; Blake & Moulton, 1969; Burke, 1978; Campbell, Campbell & Assoc., 1988; Cooper & Robertson, 1988; Dunnette, 1976; Dyer, 1976, 1987; French & Bell, 1973; Grant, 1980; Herzberg, Mausner & Snyderman, 1959; Miles, 1975; Lawrence & Lorsch, 1969; Likert, 1961; Lippit, Watson & Westley, 1958; Margulies & Raia, 1972; McCormick & Ilgen, 1980; Miles, 1975; Nevis, 1987; Schein, 1965, 1969, 1987; Strauss, 1976; Thompson, 1967.

7. See Engdahl, Walsh & Goldbeck, 1980; Follman, 1978; Kiefhaber & Goldbeck, 1979; McLean, 1974; Noland, 1973; Schmitz, 1981, 1983.

2

Roots and Branches

The uncreative mind can spot wrong answers, but it takes a creative mind to spot wrong questions.

Antony Jay (1968)[1]

THE CASE OF THE SURPRISE BONUS

Toward the end of a consulting day, the company president casually asks the consulting psychologist, "Before you go, I just wanted to ask you if you've got anything to say about bonus systems. I am probably going to put one in, and I was wondering if you had anything to say about the pro's and con's of surprising people with their bonuses or letting them know in advance what the bonus would be based on. I am inclined toward surprising them because I think that somehow the fact that it would not be expected would make people feel better about it."

After a long and hectic day of consulting, the psychologist feels pretty worn out and talked out. His first thought is, "That's a really good question." He then wonders, "Is it a waste of a good reinforcer?" He then muses, "Then again, maybe the spontaneity of a surprise might lead people to just *feel* better about the organization." What follows next in the psychologist's consciousness is a scattering of associations:

But there is no real one-to-one correspondence between incentive systems and behavior.

Make them feel better to what purpose?

Maybe there has been a study . . .

8

Is a surprise noncontingent?

What does he really want?

What is the problem?

There is something . . . not quite . . . about this "making feel good" . . .

How *would* they feel?

The psychologist then resorts to a familiar device to buy time, to sit back and get the lay of the land, to figure out what is going on: "Can you tell me a little more about your thinking on this?"

As the conversation progresses, the psychologist is faced with some important choices that will determine the direction and the helpfulness of the conversation. He could choose, for example, to try to find out what it really is that the president wants to accomplish and then help the president design his compensation system in such a way as to achieve that result. Many studies have been done that bear on the issue (see Deci, 1972; Guzzo, 1979; Lawler, 1966, 1971, 1981; Schwab & Dyer, 1973; Steers & Porter, 1979; Terborg & Miller, 1976). The psychologist is an *expert* on human motivation and reward systems. The psychologist can help the president design a system that reinforces both the attainment of certain goals as well as the particular behaviors that are necessary along the way.

Alternatively, it may be that the executive in question is naive regarding behavioral causality, in which case the psychologist might help him look at the variety of rewards— tangible and intangible—that the organization could provide. It is likely, for example, that the manager may be overlooking *non*monetary rewards in his day-to-day management of his people, that he is failing to consciously try to meet people's individual needs. Even the most sophisticated managers sometimes forget that individuals have needs. Such a conversation might ultimately turn into a discussion about organizational *value systems,* and how the president can build his constituency by viewing leadership as more than just bonus systems, how his choice can affect how he is perceived and his overall effectiveness. All executives know these things at some level, but most tend to overlook the omnipresence of psychological causation.

The psychologist asks for more information because he is looking for a clue as to what the *real* problem is. Why does the need for a bonus system spring to mind at this particular moment? The clinician assumes that the initial question may have little to do with whatever the real problem is, and he views the question not as an opportunity to answer, but as an opportunity to explore. Is the president frustrated because he has seen some evidence that the organization is not pulling together? Since he has been at the job for only five months, is he feeling that he has failed to gain the acceptance of his constituency and, if so, is this failure real or imagined?

The company was a new venture, and it was only three weeks before this conversation that the carefully selected sales force had been sent out to sell. Earlier that day, the president had indicated his disappointment in the lack of any immediate results, but he also indicated that this early in the game it was no cause for alarm. He had, in fact, predicted a very slow start. The psychologist had been reassured earlier in the day by the president's competent and mature ability to maintain a balanced perspective while owning up to his sense of disappointment. But, as the president now speaks, it becomes apparent that his reasoning regarding bonus systems seems rather mushy—especially for an otherwise highly articulate individual.

The psychologist now recalls some of the themes underscored as a result of the personal psychological evaluation conducted with the executive—for example, his tendency to seek out the acceptance of others when he feels insecure and his action-oriented reactivity that often serves him well unless he feels out of control and loses perspective. The president, then, is likely to be considering acting for the sake of acting, to provide himself with the illusion of control in the face of uncertainty, and to do so through a gesture of acceptance-seeking.

ROOTS AND BRANCHES

The management psychologist, then, takes it all in—level upon level—and tries to sort it all out. The idea is not only to get to the "root" of the issue, but to assume that issues have many "roots" and many "branches," some beneath the surface and some above the surface. The clinician's job is to help the client to *search,* to *discover,* and to *work through* the issue at whatever level is appropriate for that client at that particular time, depending on the client's psychological readiness. The goal is to free up the client so that new manifestations of old problems are not dealt with as though they are being encountered for the first time. The consultant helps the person connect broader themes in order to learn from the past (see Bazerman, 1986; Goleman, 1985; Greenwald, 1980; Snyder & Smith, 1982).

The psychologist helps the manager to recognize that the nature and force of his call for action speaks more to his discomfort at having to wait, virtually helplessly, as the important returns come in than it speaks to the issue of incentive systems. Now, the manager perhaps can avoid the costly distraction of an irrelevant excursion or at least make a decision based on what truly is relevant. Furthermore, the manager is helped to view a few more of the features of the surface topography of his adjustment style—to discern a few new snags in his behavioral terrain. The manager is then better positioned to use these surface snags as referents with which to triangulate within his own psychological space and to invite deeper insight. The psychologist helps the manager become aware of his unrealistic expectations for himself, and how he allowed his most optimistic predictions to become the standard by which he measured himself, how he stuck to those predictions, became frustrated, and then distracted himself from his mission. The clinician helps the manager become better attuned to his own subjective experience of himself, of others, and of situations, in order to better manage his inner emotional life, to free himself of subjective distortion, and to broaden his transparent consciousness of the experience of living.

The clinician refuses to take things at face value and does not overcommit to assumed hypotheses lest the process of revealing errors and possibilities be suppressed. Instead, he or she tries to simultaneously consider *all* levels. The choice of which levels to address and how to address them are strategic psychotherapeutic decisions based on the readiness of the client as well as practical and contextual considerations. The psychologist is there to help the manager make good decisions and to grow personally. The psychologist needs to weigh the manager's ability to handle issues and to implement solutions. Since most organizational decisions involve people, the psychologist must consider the culture of the organization and its readiness to incorporate change.

SELF-SCRUTINY

Through all of this the consultant must be looking at his or her own biases and sorting them out. For example, the consultant could be awed by the president's competent demeanor, or his high status and salary, or the consultant might be afraid to fail to give him the compensation solution originally requested. Or, the consultant may be experiencing his or her own sense of helplessness—parallel to the manager's—as a need to "do something *now*."

Additionally, the psychologist needs to be aware of how each of his or her choices of response defines the nature of the therapeutic relationship. For example, to the extent that the psychologist responds as an expert in reinforcement systems, other roles (sounding board, therapist, etc.) are potentially diminished. The clinician attempts to see how each little bit of the professional's behavior dynamically shapes the therapeutic contract, the developmental opportunities for the client, and the clinician's future role.

It is this constant awareness and scrutiny of the *process* that is characteristic of the art of the clinician. The clinician, then, simultaneously analyzes the process, searches within himself or herself, looks for meaning in tiny transactions, resists the urge to rush toward clarification, takes for granted the juxtaposition of many levels, and looks for the broader impact

& knowledge of effective leadership style & technique

of the person on the social system and the social system on the person. All of this is filtered through the clinician's grasp for the way changes in individuals and in systems take place.

Clinicians typically adopt relatively reactive and opportunistic therapeutic styles. They journey with the client, following more than leading and wondering what they will sense next. The practice of management psychology requires a fast-on-the-feet resourcefulness because of the simultaneity of multiple agenda and levels. Furthermore, the day itself is often unplanned and the opportunities are often unforeseen. There is a need for the clinician to stand his or her ground, to lean on an inner core of identity, and to maintain independence all the more fiercely as the consultant aligns with the interpersonal ebb and flow.

3

Structuring a Trusting Consulting Relationship

Do not speak of secret matters in a field that is full of little hills.
Hebrew Proverb

Models are made to stimulate, not to confine. The models in this chapter and in the rest of the book are ones that have evolved over many years of practice. I deviate from them only with caution, not because they are sacred, but because they are useful.

Just as in psychotherapy, the nature of the initial client contact plays a large part in determining the ultimate course of the relationship. Expectations are created not only regarding consulting activities and outcomes, but also about how the consultant should be perceived and related to by the people within the client organization.

DEFINING THE PRESENTING PROBLEM

The contact person—usually the president of the company—typically has a problem to present that "needs fixing." He or she may have discussed the problem with a trusted attorney or, perhaps, a golfing partner who is the chief executive of another organization, and that person may have made the referral to the consultant or to the consultant's firm. Less frequently, the client has had experience with psychological consultants, and has a problem that fits with the client's conception of what management psychologists do. Given the great variety of approaches and interconnecting disciplines, the client's preconceptions will often vary significantly from a given consultant's approach. In a few cases, the client will know what you are about and may even be calling you in without a specific presenting problem because he or she has seen the value of psychological consulting in the past.

The presenting problem can take many shapes:

1. The president may be looking toward retirement and/or selling the business and may want help in choosing a successor or a strategy for succession.

2. The president may be frustrated by the failures of people who have previously been hired and may be seeking psychological studies of candidates to break the pattern.

3. Two or more departments or people may be in conflict and, thereby, preventing progress toward an important goal, and the president may be seeking "something to increase teamwork around here."

4. A manager may be underperforming and the president wants the psychologist to work with the manager to overcome apparent emotional obstacles to achievement.

5. A manager may be producing brilliant results but at the cost of great conflict and disruption, and the president may wish the psychologist to help that manager to be more constructive.

6. The president may be frustrated by the inability of the company to change its mentality as market conditions are changing. For example, the president may be frustrated because the company has not been able to get its front-line people to be more truly customer service oriented, or more truly quality conscious. The president may ask for a customer service training program, or for a quality consciousness program, or for advice as to how to proceed.

7. The company's attorney may have suggested bringing in a psychologist because in the course of labor

negotiations much dissension, resentment against management, or lack of communication between management and labor may have surfaced.

8. A board member may have suggested the need for restructuring the organization or for upgrading talent in order to facilitate the company's rapid growth prospects, and the president calls the psychologist in to assess the situation.

9. The company's marketing strategy consultant may have become frustrated by the organization's inability to change course in the face of obvious market conditions and may suggest that the problem is in the organizational structure and that a psychologist should be called in.

10. In a family business there may be feuding between various relatives with divergent roles and stakes in the business, and the psychologist may be called in to help achieve family peace and to facilitate sound business decision making.

11. The company may be hiring a key executive and is concerned about some questionable experiences or references, and therefore calls the psychologist "for testing."

As with most client problems that present themselves to psychotherapists, there usually is more to the problem than meets the client's eye. The psychologist's job is to address the immediate problems as well as the factors that maintain them and those that predispose the organization toward them. As the initial meeting progresses, I try to make it clear to the client that I consult in such a way as to address the root causes of problems as well as their immediate manifestations.

In most cases, I explain to the client that the best way for me to understand what is behind the problem is by getting to know each of the key people in the organization as individuals through a process involving in-depth psychological studies and feedbacks. Most of the time, with an understanding of group members as individuals, it is possible to see why they have organized the way they have, why they interact in the way they do, and, then, why *this* group of individuals tends to encounter *these* types of problems.

I generally begin a consulting relationship, then, with a series of psychological studies with key individuals, starting with the chief executive. The psychological study is an in-depth assessment of a person's abilities, predispositions, strengths, and weaknesses. I usually insist that the chief executive go through a study first, since he or she sets the tone for the organization as well as for my relationship with the organization. Participation by anyone else is voluntary and strictly confidential. It is much easier for the chief executive to promote the potential value of the experience having already personally undertaken the process.

The tradition I follow defines the client as the individual with whom we are transacting at any moment. Our allegiance, then, is directly to the individual and only indirectly to a corporate or organizational entity. Confidentiality is, there-fore, absolute, and the best interests of each individual are the foremost considerations. Naturally, this is much easier to say than to do and, ultimately, the consultant's integrity deter-mines the success with which true allegiance to the individual is maintained.

I further explain to the chief executive that each individual will receive written and oral feedback on his or her psycho-logical study. The welfare and development of each individual is the major emphasis of the study. The study is primarily an investment in the individual and only incidentally a potential source of information about the individual. Therefore, the individual will have the option of granting the psychologist permission to share the results up the chain of command. Access is very rigidly controlled. In addition, as a general rule, no one gains access to another person's report until they have gone through the process themselves—in part because then it is much easier to understand the report's derivations and limitations.

A SPECIAL RELATIONSHIP

I want the client to understand that I am respectful of the client's presenting problem, and that I intend to deal with it.

But I also want the client to understand from the *outset* that I have my own professional needs: I need time, the client's attention and patience; I need strict adherence to the certain rules of confidentiality and sound procedure; my distaste for quick-fixes needs to be indulged; and my own and my profession's ethical standards need to be respected. I make no formal contract and provide no lecturing or written materials about my professional needs, but as issues arise, and through the way I conduct myself, I try to convey that *this* consulting relationship is *different,* that only through the trust people are willing to grant me can I be effective.

In due course I make it clear that I mean what I say about the confidentiality being absolute: that it is not my purpose to be a conduit of information, except in proscribed circumstances (such as attitude surveys and certain psychological studies) where my role and purposes and the degree of confidentiality are clear in advance; that my written and oral communications about individuals need to be safeguarded and to be communicated only to those to whom permission has been granted; that I need to be kept in the loop so as to consistently monitor the ways in which my inputs are being disseminated and interpreted.

I believe it is essential to create a real and apparent sacrosanct aura surrounding the consulting relationship, and this aura can be maintained in many small but significant ways. How the confidentiality of psychological studies is safeguarded in the organization and at the consultant's office, the degree to which an attitude of constructive respect for individuals is emphasized in handling psychological studies and in other areas of the consultant's behavior—these modes of conduct and the consistency with which they are upheld define the strength of the bridge of trust between the consultant and the individual. Similarly, what information does and does not appear on monthly bills, who knows what about whom the psychologist sees, the terms on which the psychologist consults to particular individuals, and the discreetness with which the psychologist's office handles even simple requests for information will all play parts in determining the individual's willingness to be truly vulnerable.

Having followed other psychologists into client organizations after the previous relationships were terminated or allowed to die, I have seen how, in spite of many valuable contributions, the failure to maintain long-term trust can erode the relationship. If the consultant's purposes are not explicit and clarified in advance, or if the client is defined as the organization and not the individual, or even if that is the perception though not the reality, organizations have a way of finding and reifying blemishes in the consultant. There always seems to come a time when it is politically convenient to use such accrued blemishes as leverage to get the consultant out of the way. Occasionally, I am told that I have just "passed the test," that information was leaked to me for no other reason than to trace its dispersal like radioactive iodine in radiology. The potential for organizations to exploit people is great enough and one's career is important enough that such precaution is not quite as paranoid as it might seem. Good managers tend to be skilled avoiders of adversity, and they are apt to look the gift horse consultant in the mouth lest the horse be Trojan.

In addition, the psychologist, by playing out values that include caring about and respecting the individual, models how such respect can be conveyed while still meeting organizational needs. Although very few individuals actually take advantage of their opportunity to refuse to share their studies with management, they treasure their right to do so, and they tend to find it easier to *join* with their dignity intact. Certainly, there are implicit pressures toward compliance over which the consultant cannot exercise control; however, the eventual trust in the consultant will be proportional to the degree to which the consultant minimizes coercion.

A TYPICAL PRESENTING PROBLEM: THE MALEVOLENT PRODUCTION MANAGER

At the conclusion of a social gathering the president of a $100 million engineering company waved over the management psychologist whose acquaintance he had made about a year before. "I was wondering if you guys could recommend a seminar for one of my people. He is a very bright and capable fellow, but he is also a bull in a china shop with a chip on his shoulder a mile wide. He is my vice president of production, and he has managed to wreck a $2 million joint program between production and engineering."

The psychologist responded, "If *he* thinks he has a problem, and *if* he has reasonably accurately defined his problem, and *if* he wants to work on it, and *if* you can find a good seminar, and *if* that seminar happens to click with him when he attends it, then maybe you'll see some kind of change in his behavior. But even if he could change as he needs to, and even if he could maintain that change, he still has to come back to the real-world environment and to the same issues and people that predisposed him to act that way in the first place."

The company president smiled and said, "Somehow I am beginning to get the idea that you and I may be about to have a consulting relationship."

The pair met a week later at the president's office and discussed the way the relationship would go, beginning with psychological studies of the president and the six vice presidents who reported to him, including the vice presidents of production and of engineering. The president, Mike, would introduce the program at the next Monday management meeting, and emphasize that it was a voluntary and confidential program designed to enable each of them to become more effective personally and professionally. He would assure them that they need not share their psychological studies with him, but that should they wish to, his purpose would be to better understand them, their needs, and what he must do to be a more effective manager for them. He would indicate that he would start the ball rolling by going through the psychological study and feedback process himself, and he would leave it to the six vice presidents to schedule their own times with the psychologist at their own convenience. (The psychologist had specifically asked that the vice presidents of production and of engineering not be singled out to go first.) Additionally, the president would indicate that if the group felt that the process was useful, the psychologist would continue on a regular basis to work further with top management as well as to extend the process through other levels of the organization.

Two Conflicting Styles

The vice president of production, Joe, was as bright and as volatile as his boss had described him to be. He was a scrapper who deeply feared being trod upon, as in many ways he had been in his youth. He was intolerant, impatient, over-bearing, overcontolling, tactless, egocentric, and abrasive. He was also deeply ambitious, genuinely concerned about his people, strategic, progressive, hardworking, prime-moving, and able to make things happen with a deep and well-coordinated sense of purpose. He had fought bitterly, some-times in public, over issues of turf, control, and strategy with the vice president of engineering, Frank. Joe and Frank had been mandated to install a new system, which both agreed, in principle, was essential to future profitability. Installation of the system required reorganizing both teams and reapportion-ing responsibilities, with fairly intricate coordination and mutual orchestration.

The entire program had to be abandoned because of intense conflicts, costly delays, and an inability to maintain current operations as the project was being implemented. It was known that Joe had led his people in a variety of maneuvers that disrupted the progress of the project. On a number of occasions he had verbally assaulted Frank, as well as several of the engineering managers. Joe's own people in manufactur-ing recognized most of his faults and, in fact, had been at one time or another victimized by his authoritarian attitude. Nevertheless, they felt that Joe and they had been basically in the right, and they saw the engineers as unrealistic, conde-scending, rigid, naive, and incompetent robots who unthink-ingly did whatever they were told, and who were more concerned with "saving their butts" than with producing a better product.

Frank, like his counterpart in production, was very bright. He too was deeply dedicated to the organization's purposes and to his own career advancement. However, in contrast to Joe, Frank was a very well-mannered person who carried himself with a great deal of poise, composure, and apparent evidence of "good upbringing." On the other hand, he was extremely distant, insensitive, intellectualized, and disdainful of anyone with as little refinement as Joe. To his subordinates, Frank was very sincere but hard to read, brilliant but hard to follow intellectually, and demanding but uninvolved and uninspiring. His people regarded the manufacturing people as a group of fairly nasty, stubborn, and stupid people who had been brainwashed by "little Hitler" (their name for Joe).

Even without the corroboration of subordinates and peers, the opposing characters of Joe and Frank explained much of what had happened. Both had operated fairly effectively as long as there was little need for mutual trust and cooperation, and as long as neither's turf was threatened. But when the situation changed, and stresses occurred, their styles of communication and conflict resolution clashed disastrously. Each clash resulted in the creation and perpetuation of ripples upon ripples of vicious circles. Frank's distant communication style fueled Joe's suspicions which, in turn, led Joe to block Frank's initiatives. Joe's blocking confirmed Frank's contempt which, in turn, led Frank to avoid or finesse Joe. Frank's failure to confront Joe proved to Joe that Frank was "pulling something," thus justifying his counterattack, and so on.

A Distanced President

Mike, the president, did not understand this underlying turbulence between his two subordinates. What he saw was Joe's acting out and Frank's sometimes rigidity, but he did not understand how one led to the other. Mike's approach was to leave the two to work it out between themselves, and this deprived them of escalation as a means of defusing or resolving conflicts. Had they been more mature, more competent communicators, or less "hooked" by the other's style, the president's course might have been a noble one. In the present instance, however, it only made matters worse. As each conflict occurred, Joe and Frank became more and more angry with each other. Each saw his counterpart's irrationality as "getting me in trouble with Mike" for not having the managerial skill to successfully resolve the issues.

The situation was exacerbated by Mike's preference for the global view over the details. Since many of the issues that separated his subordinates were highly complex and often technical, Mike's failure to get intimately involved with the issues kept him from shedding any useful light on them or from putting the issues into a larger perspective. Additionally, since the intensity of Joe's behavior was so clearly out of line, Mike had tended to label Joe alone as a "problem child." This labeling only exacerbated Joe's frustration and heightened his intensity level. It also made him more determined to put Frank "in his place" and to prove to Mike what a fool he was and that it was Frank's obstructionism and poor attitude that were causing the conflicts, not Joe's "justified" reactions. Similarly, the more Mike held Joe accountable, the less he held Frank accountable, and the less sincere were his demands upon Frank to work it out with Joe. As he was held less and less accountable, Frank grew increasingly disdainful of Joe and more sure of the impossibility of working things out. Frank came to regard the problem as one of Mike's indecisiveness, since Mike, after all, was allowing a "maniac" to roam free.

Tying It Together

It became apparent that all three individuals were contributing in their own ways to the problem at hand. It was also clear that the three conflicting styles had to contribute to a wide range of other apparently unrelated issues. The initial focus of consulting was to help each individual see his own part in the present problems and to relate his behavioral style to deeper issues within. The consultant stressed to each that their styles generalized to a variety of other situations and roles of both a personal and vocational nature.

Within the context of feedback and follow-up discussions, each individual was encouraged to explore in greater breadth the surface topography of his own response style and in greater depth his own underlying emotional terrain. As this occurred, each man was forced to grapple with a stronger sense of his own accountability. Within the limits of confidentiality, the psychologist also helped them understand why and how the things one did affected the others, how the messages that were actually received were different from the ones intended, and how misinterpreted stylistic differences exaggerated frustrations. Each manager developed greater respect for the importance of understanding individual differences, as well as more tolerance and willingness to psychologically legitimize the differences he found. Further, as the psychologist guided them through these issues and helped them make changes toward greater personal and organizational effectiveness, the psychologist's own role and its potential organizational impact became clearer.

The process followed along similar lines for the other four vice presidents. At this point, the management group decided to engage the consultant on a regular basis, with a fairly loose mandate to continue the process of psychological studies and feedbacks at the next levels of the organization. While continuing to consult with those who completed the process, the psychologist would be ready to provide assistance generally as problems and opportunities arose. In addition, the organization decided to make the services of the consultant's firm available to managers involved in the hiring process. Applicants' psychological characteristics would be assessed prior to hiring to determine the extent of fit between the applicant, the psychological job description, the organizational culture, and the hiring manager.

In the course of the consulting relationship, the psychologist played many roles in many contexts, including giving seminars on interviewing, stress management, and human development; working with groups to build teams and enhance communication; taking and analyzing attitudinal data; working with groups to deal with the ramifications of the data; serving as a mental health crisis and referral service; and consulting on issues from organizational structure, to acquisitions and mergers, to compensation plans. Despite these numerous roles, the foundation of the consulting relationship was the process of evaluations, feedback, and subsequent consulting to the individual and his or her manager. The cement that held the consulting relationship together was both in defining the *individual* as the client and maintaining confidentiality.

4

The Psychological Study

The personal commitment of a man to his skill, the intellectual commitment and the emotional equipment working together as one, has made the Ascent of Man.

Bronowski (1973)[1]

The psychological study is to a normal population what the clinical assessment is to an abnormal population. The emphasis of the psychological study is on health rather than pathology, and it has dramatically more wide-ranging potential. It is an in-depth, comprehensive assessment of a person's all-around functioning, and it is a starting point in developing an understanding of the person. The psychological study attempts to capture a person's capacities, styles, directions, level of emotional maturity, and the degree to which he or she capitalizes on basic potentials. It is the consultant's way of gathering a maximum of data, usefully integrating that data, and predicting future functioning.

The psychological study originated as a tool for evaluating candidates for executive positions. Companies wanted to screen-in bright and mature individuals and to screen-out those with major emotional problems or other psychological liabilities. Over time psychologists found that their evaluations could be put to good use even after a person was hired. Managers could be helped to tailor their behavior to better take into account the characteristics of the individuals they managed. Similarly, individuals could gain better control of their own behavior by deepening their understanding of themselves. The psychological study thereby evolved from a context of evaluation for selection purposes to a broader context as a managerial and developmental stimulus. This

26

transition had a profound influence on the role of the consulting psychologist. No longer was the psychologist merely a diagnostician with a specific, limited role to play at particular points in time; now the consultant maintained on-going, dynamic involvement with the organization as an active stimulus for change (see Flory, 1965). These developments, taking place around World War II, parallelled similar changes in defining clinical psychology as dealing not only with clinical assessment but also with therapeutic change.

The focus of psychological studies also increased in breadth as psychology itself broadened its focus. In addition to focusing on and assessing intelligence and emotional disorder, psychological studies in the 1940s and 1950s increasingly began to look at motivation and to distinguish among kinds of *positive* motivation.[2] Similarly, as psychology moved from models of human behavior based on personality deviance toward those emphasizing psychological health and self-actualization[3], psychological studies, in turn, looked at individuals within the context of normal human growth and development.

The psychological study, then, is an attempt to assess people from a holistic, psychological perspective in order to provide meaningful feedback to individuals and/or their prospective or current managers. It serves many purposes: to describe *and predict* performance; as a mirror on one's life and a stimulus for personal growth; as a developmental manual for a person's manager; as an inventory of organizational talent; and, as the beginning of a trusting relationship with the consultant.

WHAT TO LOOK FOR IN PSYCHOLOGICAL STUDIES

In doing a psychological study there are a number of objectives to achieve. The consultant needs to understand the individual as well as possible, to get under the individual's skin, and to relate to the individual's sense of self (see Epstein, 1980; Schlenker, 1985; Wells & Marwell, 1976; Wylie, 1979), sense of his or her interpersonal world, and sense of his or her boundaries and extensions. The consultant tries to determine the person's fears, hopes, aspirations, and values. It is an opportunity to help an individual articulate and reflect on his or her life and to help the individual to feel understood. It is a vehicle for gaining a sense of the individual's developmental flow and momentum in order to be able to follow out into the future the individual's life lines.[4] The object is to help the individual see where his or her present steps are likely to lead and to offer the individual choices.

By looking for congruities and incongruities—between potential and achievement, aspiration and potential, feeling and thinking, accountability and the perception of it, the verbal and the nonverbal, words and deeds, words and words—the possibility for later trying to stimulate the individual to better align is fostered.

The psychological study seeks to gauge the caliber of the person, the inner fiber, the person's "size." In a Maslowian sense (Maslow, 1970), it attempts to determine the characteristic level at which the person operates, the person's degrees of freedom, levels of maturity and gratification, and the person's emotional flexibility and openness. It looks at the individual's capacity for reciprocity, for establishing and maintaining constituencies, and for expressing generosity and genuine caring.

A person's assets, liabilities, and options are assessed in order to better predict his or her future. By understanding the past and present *situational* realities with which the person is confronted, it is possible to gauge the supports and strains (see Shaver, 1984; Snyder & Ford, 1987) and the person's ability to cope with and without them. Similarly, I try to understand the person as a *physiological* being.[5] An evaluation of the way a person has perceived and managed the choice points and crisis points of life helps assess the realism, purposefulness, self-accountability, foresight, initiative, courage, and emotional congruence of the key choices. This, in turn, makes it feasible to point out what he or she can do and what management can do to change the probable results. (See Appendix A, "What to Look for in Psychological Studies," which details in much greater depth questions to keep in mind when conducting a psychological study and composing the report.)

Eliciting the Data

In order to answer all of these questions, an in-depth, face-to-face interview is essential. A thorough developmental history reveals the influences, the risks, the advantages, the limitations, the barriers, the crises, and the choice points with which the individual has had to cope. Characteristic coping styles emerge as well as the overall effectiveness of these styles for the individual's long-term adaptation to and gratification from life. Open-ended, projective-style questions help the interviewer align with the individual's own *perception* of events as well as the past and present *emotional response* to those events. These perceptions help to illuminate the person's own sense of active involvement and accountability for managing the ups and downs of life. It is helpful to learn how these perceptions and emotions evolved and shaped the individual and his or her adjustment styles, how they have changed over time, and how much insight the individual has into his or her personality and its development.

Questions are designed to view the person through a variety of experiential windows—educational, familial, marital, social, communal, cultural, vocational, physiological, recreational, and economic—to obtain the fullest possible picture. Questions which force a person to make value judgments or perceptual judgments can also be very revealing:

- What (subject, teacher, job, boss, life event) did you like (best, least)?

- How would you describe your (mother, father, sibling, teacher, boss, friend, spouse, child, job, organization, management style, strengths, shortcomings, self, etc.)?

- Where have you received the most (praise, criticism, success, failure, satisfaction, frustration)?

Primarily as means of confirmation and integration, projective questions are of additional value:

- If you had three wishes . . .

- If you could meet anyone in history . . .

- What kind of animal . . .

- If you could relive your life . . .

A source on clinical interviewing would also be helpful here (see Fear, 1980; Morgan & Cogger, 1980; Pruyser, 1979; Sundberg, 1977).

Various tests (see Anastasi, 1982; Ghiselli, 1973; Lezak, 1982; McReynolds, 1975; Most & Glazer, 1983; Wiggins, 1973) may be used as an adjunct to a clinical interview in order to account for more variance, to affirm the objectivity of the interviewer, and to alert the interviewer to issues that may otherwise not be uncovered. Unfortunately, some practitioners overuse tests and overinterpret test results. They may do so because they lack comfort or skill in interpreting interview information, because they lack faith in their own clinical judgments, because they are stingy with their time, or because they have become overly impressed with testing technology's seeming ability to put people in neat little boxes. In contrast, I would suggest that testing *per se* can not compensate for lack of quality interviewing and sound interpretation. Tests may yield results that stimulate executives in certain areas; however, their inherent limitations encourage simplistic and temptingly mechanistic conceptions of psychological causation and discourage holistic perspectives which respect the uniqueness and complexity of individuals. Nice little boxes with nice little labels provide people with false comfort and tend to retard exploration. With the advent in the 1980s of the convenience of computerized test interpretation, test-based superficiality increased by an order of magnitude (Eyde & Kowal, 1987; Fowler & Butcher, 1987; Huba, 1987; Moreland, 1987; Most, 1987).

A Useful Framework

One variant of a widely used framework for organizing psychological study results views the person from six perspectives:

1. *Intellectual Characteristics*—Degree and kinds of intelligence, cognitive styles, and the degree to which an individual works up to capacity.

2. *Emotional Characteristics*—Emotional stability, maturity, modes of adjustment, ego strength, core values, degree of integration, stamina, etc.

3. *Motivational Characteristics*—Degree of drive, psychological needs, etc.

4. *Insights into Self and Others*—Flexibility, objectivity, self-scrutiny, defensiveness, receptivity, sensitivity, perceptiveness, psychological-mindedness, empathy, etc.

5. *Interpersonal Characteristics*—Adaptability, dominance, friendliness, cooperativeness, tact, poise, supportiveness, degree of intimacy, etc.

6. *Vocational Characteristics*—Technical skills, leadership skills, ability to organize, coordinate, direct, plan, and take charge, managerial style, organizational strengths and shortcomings, etc. This section highlights the implications the foregoing material has for on-the-job performance, for person-job fit, and for ways of shaping context and environment to best suit the individual. (Please see Appendix A for elaboration.)

This framework has the advantage of starting with deeper personality characteristics, moving through the bridge of insight, and ending with the social and vocational manifestations of personality in behavior. Since psychological development occurs on many levels—emotional growth, development of insight, and behavioral change—it is important to illuminate each of the levels as well as their interconnectedness. If people are to grow increasingly accountable for their own development, and if managers are to hold themselves increasingly accountable for the development of their subordinates, then the individual must be presented as a multilayered whole and not as a label on a box. Therefore, the six perspectives need to be conceived as overlapping, integrated, and consistent. For reasons of clarity, many practitioners divide their psychological study reports into six categories corresponding to the six perspectives. Others avoid subdivision because of the danger of oversimplification and overcategorization.

THREE VARIANTS OF PSYCHOLOGICAL STUDIES

As a Developmental Stimulus

The developmental evaluation helps refresh a person's working memory of his or her experience of life. It is an attempt to help a person take stock, to reassess present directions and coping styles, to increase personal alignment, and to gain insight into the person's relationship with others within an organizational context. It is also an opportunity for the individual to enter into a very personal relationship with the consultant and to learn something of the rewards of self-revelation. Assuming permission is granted to feed back to the individual's boss, there is a distinct opportunity to help the organization better frame the individual's working environment.

The developmental psychological study provides the psychologist with an opportunity to understand the key players, their competencies, their shortcomings, their biases, their attitudes toward others, their unexpressed needs, their values, their hidden agenda, their ways of dealing with obstacles, and their ways of subjectively experiencing their inner and outer realities. The process of clinical assessments provides a window into an organization's core potentials and pitfalls. The perspective gained illuminates facets of organizational reality that remain obscure when viewed from more traditional organizational perspectives such as financial, strategic, marketing, or structural windows.

The psychological study provides individuals with a nonjudgmental mirror of personal reality that attempts to stimulate them to take stock, to see in reflection the coursing of their personal waters, to look again at their potentials, and to reappraise their dreams. The process of evaluation and feedback allows individuals, if they are ready, to unfreeze; and, as individuals unfreeze, systems unfreeze; and as systems unfreeze, symptoms change and growth occurs.

If people grant permission to share psychological studies with their managers, the recipient managers can do a better job of bringing out the best in the people who report to them. They can learn to use a nonjudgmental, respectful language that transforms illegitimate frustrations into challenging puzzles of possibility. As managers work on these areas, their own senses of empowerment—and, therefore, of self-accountability—grow, and they are increasingly stimulated, often without consciousness of it, to tend to their own psychological gardens.

The process of psychological studies and feedbacks seeds a trusting consulting relationship. It allows the psychologist to demonstrate authenticity, insightfulness, objectivity, confidentiality, and usefulness to each individual at a personal level. The individual is forced to reexamine preconceptions about psychology as fuzzy-minded, impractical, esoteric, gushingly emotional, hopelessly diffuse, or concerned only with embarrassing and irrelevant inner mysteries. The psychologist begins to be seen as a helper, an enabler, and a reducer of uncertainty, whose primary allegiance is to the fostering of human dignity and human potential. The individuals begin to see the psychologist as a person who can be consulted as problems arise, and who extracts little price for vulnerability.

The process of feedbacks and psychological studies begins an evolving process of elevating the organization's cultural consciousness of psychological reality. As this process evolves, managers become more and more psychologically

aware and psychologically focused, and this increased awareness ultimately yields humaneness. Managers begin to understand psychological causation more and to label and judge
less. Their sense of developmental *time* expands. They
increasingly see their own actions as discreet units of impact
that can be applied toward long-term growth and not just
short-term gain. They increasingly see human assets as
tangible capital to be mined and nurtured, and managerial
inputs as investments. They become more tolerant of individual differences and more appreciative of diverse realities.
What begins as new and uncomfortable eventually finds its
way into the organization's collective memory and self-
identity. The psychologist knows that the impact of consulting
can be sustained when the psychologist is no longer credited,
as the memories and expectations are passed along, and the
self-examining process has been internalized by the people of
the organization.

In the Evaluation of Outside Candidates

Here the consultant serves a vital quality control function in
the process of selecting individuals to become the future brick
and mortar of the organization. The consultant predicts how
the applicant's characteristics *fit* with the "psychological job
description," the working group and company culture, and the
prospective manager's management style. Although confidentiality regarding personal details may be granted, the hiring
company, and not the individual, is the client. Yet, in most
cases, there is a strong concordance between what is in the
company's best interests and what is in the applicant's best
interests, at least to the extent that the consultant accurately
predicts the applicant's future success and effectiveness if
hired by the organization.

With Applicant-Employees Who Seek Promotion or Transfer

This situation blends characteristics of both of the above
scenarios. In some respects, most employee developmental
evaluations serve a purpose of evaluating future potential

and, in this sense, fall into the same category. The employee should, however, have the right to refuse to share the psychological study with management, since it is the individual who is the primary client. Furthermore, should the individual grant permission to feed back and share the report with management, only those directly in the chain of command should be involved. Nevertheless, there is a coercive element in the situation, since refusal to share the evaluation with management may well result in the loss of a promotion or a desired transfer. Therefore, the sensitivity, subtlety, and integrity with which the consultant handles this situation can have an enormous impact on the quality of the trust in the consultant and in the consulting relationship. Even so, it is sometimes impossible to juxtapose an effective counseling relationship with an evaluative relationship; it may be impossible to forget that your would-be counselor contributed to holding you back, and the fact that you may be persuaded that it was in your own best interests may not change the matter much.

Despite this inherent confounding of roles, I find it to be the least of all evils. As a way of reducing role conflict, it is possible to define the *organization* as the client and to settle for less trust from applicant-employees or to limit oneself to developmental evaluations only, with no feedback to the organization. However, both alternatives are unsatisfactory because they limit the consultant's ultimate value to the individuals and the organizations. In most cases, I have found that the consultant's objectivity and skill at conveying commonness of purpose can accomplish trust without sacrificing impact.

When I have seen the dual-role approach fail, it has been largely because the consultant mishandled the situation in one way or another. For example, the consultant may signal personal discomfort in walking the fine line between evaluation and counseling. Perhaps the consultant allows objectivity to be clouded by the relationship. Perhaps the consultant does not see how an individual's long-term interests are served when short-term interests are blocked, or the consultant may have difficulty persuading the individual that this is the case. Similarly, if the entire context of the consulting relationship is not maintained with a certain aura of sanctity and consistent adherence to strictures, there is a greater likelihood that the entire process will be seen as flawed. On the other hand, if the consultant is viewed as having undue influence with top management, the consultant will be treated with caution. Thus, it will be the consistency, integrity, and soundness with which the consultant frames the entire consulting relationship that determines the acceptance of the consultant's multiplicity of roles.

By far the best resolution to these dilemmas is the early use of the psychological study as a developmental tool. Rather than waiting until a position becomes available and evaluating a person as an internal candidate, it is preferable to see that person long before the job opening is an issue. With no promotion at stake, the focus then can be on what the individual can do to *get ready* for a potential opening. Not coincidentally, the organization is also in a much better "win/win" position, potentially avoiding the acrimony of rejection.

---

1. From *The ascent of man* by Jacob Bronowski, copyright © 1973 by J. Bronowski. Reprinted by permission of Little, Brown and Company.

2. See Anderson & Moore, 1959; Atkinson, 1958; Cofer & Appley, 1964; Erikson, 1950; Gellerman, 1963; Glanzer, 1958; Hall, Bowen, Lewicki & Hall, 1982; Hartmann, 1958; Hendrick, 1942; Hertzberg, Mausner & Synderman, 1959; McClelland et al., 1953; Murray, 1938, 1951, 1959; Schilder, 1942; Spence, 1983; Vroom, 1964; White, 1959, 1960.

3. See Allport, 1955; Jahoda, 1953; Kelley, 1970; Langer, 1969; Maslow, 1970, 1971; Murphy, 1958; Rogers, 1961; Tannenbaum & Davis, 1969.

4. See Baltes & Schaie, 1973; Baltes & Brim, 1981; Bond & Rosen, 1980; Bray, Campbell & Grant, 1974; Bridges, 1980; Brim, 1976; Datan & Ginsberg, 1976; Erikson, 1980; Figler, 1978; Gould, 1978; Gubrium & Buckholdt, 1977; Herr & Cramer, 1979; Kanter, 1977 (a), 1977 (b); Levinson, 1978; Lowenthal, Thurnher & Chiriboga, 1976; Norman & Scaramella, 1980; Offer & Sabshin, 1984, 1988; Osipow, Doty, & Spokane, 1985; Smelser & Erikson, 1980; Sze, 1975; Vaillant, 1977; Vondracek, Lerner, & Schulenberg, in press.

5. See Bakal, 1979; Baum & Singer, 1983; Bradley & Prokop, 1981; Chesney & Feuerstein, 1979; Gatchel & Baum, 1982; Gatchel & Baum, 1983; Genst & Genst, 1987; Goldberg, 1978; Herd & Fox, 1981; Lazarus & Folkman, 1984; Melamed & Siegel, 1988; Millon, Green & Meagher, 1982; Pomerleau & Brady, 1979; Rachman, 1980; Selye, 1976; Sternbach, 1966; Weiner, 1977.

5

The Psychological Study Report and Feedback

There is a time in every man's education when he arrives at the conviction that envy is ignorance; that imitation is suicide; that he must take himself for better, for worse, as his portion; that though the wide universe is full of good, no kernel of nourishing corn can come to him but through his toil bestowed on that plot of ground which is given to him to till.
Ralph Waldo Emerson ("Self-Reliance")

In the previous chapter we compared the psychological study to the clinical assessment. Whereas the clinical assessment is typically diagnostic with only global treatment implications, the psychological study is potentially developmental *in its own right*. In other words, not only does the clinician use the insights, but the client does too—and often the process of going through the "study" is developmental in and of itself.

To enhance trust and openness in the process of psychological studies and feedbacks, it is essential that the consultant actively convey a nonjudgmental attitude toward all people at all times and in many small ways. The psychological study report should avoid any comments that could be taken as value judgments, although this can be a difficult discipline to develop. A nonjudgmental attitude not only enhances trust and the acceptance of the consultant's multiple roles, it also has the distinct advantage of legitimizing a person's characteristics—to the person and to the person's manager. The resulting legitimacy highlights the acceptability of individual differences and the possibilities for accommodation and change.

Psychological studies are typically reported in both oral and written form. The oral presentation has the virtue of immediacy, informality, give-and-take between psychologist and evaluee, and the ease of shifting focus from broad to narrow, from abstract to concrete, and from the descriptive to the experiential. The written report allows for comprehensiveness, subtle differentiation, and a consistent message and tone for all readers. An oral report without a written one is apt to lack comprehensiveness and to be imprecise; a written report with no oral feedback does not have the advantage of further clarification and reader input, and it tends to be felt as impersonal.

THE WRITTEN REPORT

When writing a psychological study report, I assume that most people can take the truth, unvarnished and unadorned. In fact, people usually appreciate and best benefit from direct honesty. Hedging or sugar-coating tends to protect not the individual nor that person's manager, but the psychologist who fears the repercussions from honesty. It is not the truth that undermines people, but rather a judgmental or disrespectful attitude. Sugar-coating usually implies an underlying disrespect that is not only inconsistent with the truth, but with the empowerment and growth that respectful honesty seeds. Though it may not always be constructive, for the sake of truth, to grind an awareness of a person's limitations into his or her consciousness, it is usually equally nonconstructive to euphemize. Relevant shortcomings will surface, not because consultants highlight them, but because personalities reveal themselves eventually.

A sound report is balanced. It affirms the person's strengths, and in doing so, reinforces his or her readiness to consider shortcomings. An honest appraisal allows the individual to capitalize on strengths and to minimize limitations or to change course in the face of them. As Socrates said (in *Apology*), "The life which is unexamined is not worth living." For the individual's manager, an honest appraisal promotes appropriate expectations, prevents disappointment, and fosters understanding rather than name-calling.

Both evaluee and manager are challenged to confront issues as they really are rather than as misplaced diplomacy would have them be.

For example, an individual who functions around the 75th percentile intellectually needs to know that he or she will have difficulty in dealing with certain conceptual issues, especially if the individual intends to climb the management ladder. The truth may not be particularly pleasant; however, it is seldom a surprise. Furthermore, it can spur the individual to seek alternatives for career growth that place less emphasis upon high intelligence and more on characteristics that are better aligned with other strengths.

In addition, I believe that there should only be one psychological study report, that it should say all that there is to say, and that it be the one that is shared with both the individual and manager. A number of consultants do it differently. For example, some consultants write two reports, a "good" one for the individual and the "real" one for management. Others write a "real" report, but share only "safe" parts of the report with the individual. Others write a "cleaned-up" written report, but let the hard truths emerge in the oral feedback to the individual's manager. Such practices erode trust and greatly diminish the value of the report to the individual. To my way of thinking, couching the truth in one of these ways reflects the psychologist's inability to say what needs to be said in a constructive and nonjudgmental manner so it can be heard by both the manager and the individual and discussed fully by them. I find it most incongruous to see consultants preaching organizational openness on the one hand, but maintaining duplicity in the treatment of psychological studies on the other (see Gibb, 1978).

When I was new at this kind of work, I attended an American Psychological Association Preconvention Workshop led by a psychological consultant. He described an evaluation he did of an alcoholic chief executive officer. In his report he wrote nothing about alcoholism, but he did suggest that the man was better suited being a chairman of the board than a chief executive officer, as a way of persuading the man to relinquish his power. Apparently this consultant subscribed to the same philosophy as Dr. Relling in Henrick Ibsen's "The Wild Duck," who said, "Rob the average man of his life-illusion, and you rob him of his happiness at the same stroke" (see Taylor & Brown, 1988). Even if one could justify the duplicity on those grounds or on the presumed value of helping the organization get rid of an alcoholic, such an approach inevitably leads to the erosion of trust in the consultant and, consequently, of his effectiveness.

I try to envision both the individual and that individual's manager in front of me as I compose the report. It helps, therefore, to speak a language that will be common to those individuals and to avoid the comfort of jargon. It serves no purpose to bother clients with obfuscating details such as test scores, since it is the consultant who stands behind the report, not the test manufacturer. The purpose is to describe a person and not to chronicle that person's life, so I try to focus on traits, predispositions, and trends rather than historical facts, except insofar as the facts are needed to explain predispositions.

A FOCUS ON DEVELOPMENT

The psychological report is a form of therapeutic communication, and its purposes are best served with authenticity as well as appreciation for a reader's cast of mind. Additionally, the report should accommodate a reader's state of readiness to hear and benefit from what is said. For example, I try to use the person's own words whenever possible for the benefit of that individual. Using this tact provides an opportunity to set a positive and constructive tone, to offer a softer alternative to a harsh inner voice, to relabel difficulties so as to bring changing them into the realm of the possible, and to reconceptualize defenses in terms of the fears that maintain them. An interlacing of metaphor and verity may also facilitate access to that which is not conscious (see Erickson, Rossi, & Rossi, 1976).

The report helps focus the mind of the individual's manager on that individual's personal and professional development. By indicating what can be done to bring out the best in the individual and by providing a nonjudgmental language as an alternative to labels borne out of frustration, the manager may be increasingly empowered to become a positive force in that individual's life. Accordingly, the manager's sense of the scope of what it is to truly manage people expands along with his or her sense of managerial accountability. Ultimately, managers begin to see organizational progress as the fruit of long-term individual growth nurtured by the environment managers create. Furthermore, as managers face the task of development, they become more acutely aware of the importance—and the complexity—of personnel selection.

For the consultant, the psychological study is the beginning of a relationship with the individual, and its tone, its nuances, and its ramifications add texture to the relationship with both the individual and with his or her manager. For the manager, the consultant's report as well as his or her own report help to establish the trustworthiness, humanity, and helpfulness of the psychologist. Each evaluation and feedback is an opportunity for the consultant to frame a continuing relationship and to gain insight into the organization through an intimate understanding of its people. The process of psychological studies and feedbacks enables the consultant to take the pulse of the organization, to stay in touch with grapevines and informal networks of communication, and to know "what's hot." This, in turn, enables the consultant to react opportunistically in addressing a developmental issue, a conflict, or an unrecognized maladaptive organizational trend. The cumulation of psychological studies eventually provides a broad inventory of the talent—realized and unrealized—in the organization, as well as the personal, social, or cultural convergences that both define the organization and limit it. This inventory can be offered to management as a way of stimulating discussions about cultural change, improving personnel selection, individual or organizational developmental needs, or the dangers of uniformity.

DEALING WITH THE ISSUE OF PSYCHOLOGICAL FIT

Reports of psychological studies of prospective employees typically include a recommendation section which reflects the consultant's judgment of the *psychological fit* between the applicant and the job in question. In reaching this judgment, the consultant needs to consider the promotability of the candidate; the nature of the organizational culture; the characteristics of the applicant's prospective manager, co-workers, and subordinates; and barriers or special circumstances that could affect the applicant's performance, as well as the nature of the job itself. In addition, the consultant must strive as much as possible to take into account the inevitability of change and of adversity in all of these areas as well as in the applicant's personal life and in the company's fortunes. How the person will do under conditions of crisis, stress, temptation, pressure, uncertainty, disappointment, rejection, loss, failure, or lack of control are critical considerations.

Obviously, given such a formidable task, perfection in judgment of fit is unattainable. Nevertheless, the consultant's familiarity with the organization, its people, its problems, its *implicit* language, its unconscious social scripts, its ways of bridging social synapses, and its values, expectations, and conventions, gained through prior evaluations and consulting activity, sheds a good deal of light on the variance of fit. In fact, such a familiarity is the *only* way a psychologist can make a good prediction. In the total scheme of things, *describing* a candidate is comparatively easy. *Prediction,* however, demands an understanding of the situation. As people are hired, and their successes and failures are played out, the consultant recalibrates and reassesses previous judgments in order to do a better job the next time around.

Both being wrong and being right give rise to problems for the consultant. Clients can be very unforgiving when a recommended candidate fails, especially if they had not accepted full accountability for the hire in the first place. Paradoxically, the seemingly "perfect" predictions may have the unintended consequence of leading clients to view the consultant as a predictive guru and, thereby, to place too much weight upon his or her recommendations and, subtly, to accept less personal accountability for hiring decisions. A hiring manager who places too much emphasis upon the psychologist's recommendation of a candidate may tend to take the candidate's future success for granted and fail to do the hard work that is necessary once the person is on board. Furthermore, when the consultant is perceived as a guru whose pronouncements are unquestioningly heeded, concerns about the consultant's power will arise which may undermine trust. Last, the consultant needs to be vigilant in his or her awareness of the potential for dependency to undermine the objective of helping managers feel more empowered about the selection process.

I do not include a specific recommendation in the case of a current employee who is being considered for a promotion. Rather than coming down with my own bottom line, I prefer to help the individual and the manager work through the implications of the study themselves in order to encourage a fuller sense of accountability on both of their parts to accept the final decision regarding promotion or transfer. It is usually sufficient to clearly spell out the advantages and disadvantages of the fit and of its risks and benefits to the individuals and to the organization. Since the individuals involved are typically already in a relationship, this approach allows them to factor in (better than the consultant can) those issues of mutual obligation, cultural similarity (see Asante, Newmark & Blake, 1980; Daniel, 1975; Galtung, 1980, 1981; Ginges & Maynard, 1983; Price-Williams, 1975; Samovar & Porter, 1985; Spindler, 1980; Triandis, 1972), personal attraction (see Bryne, 1971), cognitive, linguistic, or perceptual commonalities (see Cole & Scribner, 1974; Gibson, 1969; Lloyd, 1972; Neisser, 1976; Nisbett & Ross, 1980; Rogers & Agarwala-Rogers, 1976; Spradley, 1972; Wyer & Scrull, 1984), or overriding shared values (see Kluckhohn & Strodbeck, 1961) which a consultant can often only obscurely perceive. On the one hand the consultant must then assume the delicate role of helping the people to guard against the blindness their subjective reactions can incur, and on the other hand, helping them to appreciate the real value of those subjective reactions.

Ending the Report with a Beginning

A concluding section can serve the purpose of crystalizing and highlighting some of the key ideas in the psychological study report. In the case of a psychological study about an outside candidate, a final section provides an opportunity to weigh the risks and benefits of the hire. Additionally, it can be a vehicle for emphasizing to the hiring manager the conditions under which the individual would perform best and worst, if hired. Implicitly then, the report reminds the manager of his or her obligations to the individual, should the person come on board. If the person needs structure, praise, stimulation, faith, tolerance—or whatever—this gives the hiring manager one more opportunity to buy in or back off, and is one more way of attempting to help the manager accept accountability for the selection decision.

With psychological studies for developmental purposes, I try to gently destabilize the person's psychological economy, to end on the up-beat and to catalyze some psychological momentum. For some people, this may involve simple suggestions of concrete actions that they can take, such as reading a certain book, pursuing an M.B.A. degree, attending a seminar, starting or stopping a particular behavior, taking up a hobby, or taking a course on finance for nonfinancial managers. Less specific suggestions might include ways of working on being more proactive, less controlling, less controlled, more assertive (see Clionsky, 1983), self-accepting, less detailistic, more introspective, more reflective, more disciplined, more initiative-taking, less reactive, more considerate, less accommodating, etc.

If it seems appropriate to the individual, and if I manage to be inspired, I may try to weave and embed a metaphor (see Barker, 1985; Billow, 1977; Evans, 1988; Gordon, 1978), or state a truism and assert its predicate (see Erickson & Rossi, 1979), or in some other way try to get behind defensive screens and beyond strictly logical cognition. As Walt Whitman said:

> Logic and sermons never convince.
> The damp of the night drives deeper into my soul.
> *(Song of Myself)*

Sometimes, a reframed echo of the person's own words may find its way back in (see Slosar, 1982). Sometimes, a trace of

Ericksonian confusion distracts long enough to irritate a person's psychological oyster (see Erickson, Rossi & Rossi, 1976; Erikson, 1980). Like all attempts at reaching whatever it is that some call the unconscious and others call the right side of the brain, sometimes it doesn't and sometimes it works. (Please see Appendix C for some examples of psychological study reports.)

GETTING THE MOST OUT OF
THE FEEDBACK SESSION

On average, the feedback session lasts about two hours. Outside of presenting the written report, I try to impose no predetermined structure or agenda. The objective is simply to be helpful. While the report is meant to stimulate and serves as a useful backdrop, I try to help the person keep a focus on his or her experience of life, and not what I have said about that experience. Like much else in the clinical approach to consulting, the feedback session is an opportunistic excursion, with the client not quite fully understanding what to expect and the clinician wondering what will "take."

Like most clinicians, I would describe myself as eclectic. I offer what seems to be appropriate to that client at that moment: listening, stimulation, evocation, interpretation, structure, direction, and, sometimes, simple advice. Since many feedback sessions will not be routinely followed up, there is more pressure than in typical psychotherapy to *achieve* something, to make something out of that particular session. It is often a rare opportunity for a psychologist to have psychotherapeutic impact with someone who would not otherwise have sought out a psychologist. Under these circumstances, I find I have to be careful, lest my own enthusiasm for the process impose too much on the client's boundaries. On the other hand, in dealing with a fairly healthy and well-motivated population of people who generally want to grow, one is less likely to stumble upon the ethical problems of imposing growth or the therapeutic problems of going too deep too soon. The major problem, then, is finding a way to make a difference in a single encounter.

Depending on the client's readiness, it is usually possible to approach the client at both a behavioral or cognitive-behavioral level (see Bandura, 1969, 1986; Beck, 1976; Goldfried & Davison, 1976; Krasner & Ullmann, 1973; Mahoney, 1974; Meichenbaum, 1977;) as well as a more psychodynamic, subjective, or intrapsychic level. The discussions can range from practical interpersonal issues at work to the developmental roots of long-standing fears and anxieties, to current family problems, to long-range career objectives, to the content and tone of a client's internal dialogue. For one client, relaxation training and specific suggestions for stress or fear reduction may be appropriate (see Cooper & Payne, 1988; Hamberger & Lohr, 1988; Lazarus & Folkman, 1984; McLean, 1974, 1979; Novaco, 1975; Schwartz, 1983). For another client, therapeutic stories might fit (see Rosen, 1982), or perhaps self-hypnosis with a pain problem (see Barber & Adrian, 1988; Bonica, 1980; Burrows, Collison, & Dennerstein, 1979; Crasilneck & Hall, 1975; Hartman, 1980; Hilgard & Hilgard, 1975; Miller, 1979; Philips, 1988; Spiegel & Spiegel, 1978). Or, I might prescribe homework *a la* Ellis (1962; 1971), or ordeals *a la* Haley (1984). When possible, I try to help clients gain greater awareness of their subjective experience of themselves and of life, for, as Bugental[1] has said:

> Our subjectivity is our true home, or natural state, and our necessary place of refuge and renewal. It is the font of creativity, the stage for imagination, the drafting table for planning, and the ultimate heart of our fears and hopes, our sorrows and satisfactions. . . . If one seeks fundamental change in his experience of being alive, that quest must, beyond question, take the seeker into the depths of his subjectivity. (Bugental, 1987, p. 4)

In short, the feedback session involves the same extensive bag of tools (see Yeager, 1983) with which the clinician is equipped in a psychotherapy session. The client's personal characteristics and concerns evoke the method. As with most psychotherapy, success depends largely on the client's readiness and on the clinician's capacity to deeply and truly connect with the client, to vulnerably experience your own subjectivity, and to freely allow your own creative therapeutic energy to help catalyze the client's movement toward the next plateau. At a minimum, the feedback session provides an opportunity for the positive affirmation of the individual.

I am often surprised by the amount of impact the feedback process can have. The fact of the psychological study itself probably has a good deal to do with the success of the feedback session. Just answering the many questions the consultant poses and taking the time to look back at one's life often catalyzes a readiness to grow. For many, the implication that the process is a growthful one is a sufficient self-fulfilling prophecy. Thus, when the logic of the self-fulfilling prophecy demands growth, people seem to find the room to grow. For some, the very decision to go through the process of the psychological study and feedback is a ritual act of readiness that predestines the positive results of the feedback session. The high drive of many executives often energizes the catalytic effect of the feedback process. For many, simply the opportunity to appreciate one's uniqueness mirrored by a respectful consultant can have a lasting impact.

Two additional constructive forces often come into play. First, specific feedback from a boss regarding desired changes can be a powerful motivator. Second, when organizations have developed a culture that expects and nurtures personal growth, people may well enter into the psychological study and feedback process with significant preexisting growth momentum. Since helping a culture to become more empowering is a central focus of a consulting relationship, this effect is most pronounced in the more enduring company-consultant relationships. These positive contributors to outcome can make consulting a real pleasure.

Even when there is little current readiness to change, there is always an opportunity to look for crevices in which to plant seeds that may sprout later or, at the very least, to try to establish the consultant as a resource to be approached at a later time of crisis or greater readiness. The consultant is most likely to be called upon in the future when change is probable, which can be efficient, albeit disorderly. Unproductive or less productive feedback sessions result from a number of factors, including: lack of trust in, respect for, or interpersonal "chemistry" with the consultant; personal rigidity, defensiveness or unreadiness; an environment that does not stimulate or encourage growth or, worse yet, one that inhibits people and leads them to choose safety over risk.

Obviously, there are no simple solutions to these problems, but they highlight the importance of developing a *long-term relationship* with a client company wherein the kind of cultural change that fosters individual growth can itself be fostered, and wherein the competence, values, and humanity of the consultant gain credibility over time. Probably the most important thing the consultant can do in the short-term is to stimulate an individual's manager to help the individual to become unstuck. Sometimes the process can operate in reverse: discussing the subordinate may be the best way to free up the boss's defenses, since it is safer to deal with someone else's problems, and often easier to muster one's sense of obligation toward another than toward one's self. The consultant then has the opportunity to deal indirectly with the subordinate through the boss and with the boss through the boss talking about the subordinate. Through the process, both are taught about what growth is—and in a very personal way.

One situation that often starts out with some strain is a feedback to a person whom the consultant evaluated and did not recommend, but who was, nevertheless, subsequently hired. Once the person is hired, I do regard it as my responsibility to make an effort to prove my own recommendation "wrong," and making this clear to the person can be a help. Most often, the person recognizes the characteristics that led to the particular recommendation, although he or she may not fully appreciate the implications for future organizational success. The goal, then, is to align with the individual, to strengthen areas in which he or she falls short, and to improve the chances of a good fit. The chances are even better if the hiring manager has genuinely committed to the same effort.

---

1. From *The art of the psychotherapist,* by J. F. T. Bugental, copyright © 1987, by W. W. Norton & Company. Reprinted by permission of the publisher.

6

Getting to the Root Causes of Organizational Problems

All the greatest and most important problems of life are fundamentally insoluble . . . They can never be solved, but only outgrown.
  This "outgrowing" proved on further investigation to require a new level of consciousness. Some higher or wider interest appeared on the patient's horizon, and through this broadening of his or her outlook the insoluble problem lost its urgency. It was not solved logically in its own terms but faded when confronted with a new and stronger life urge.

Carl Jung (*Original Blessings*)

As an outgrowth of the continuing process of psychological studies and feedbacks to employees and their managers, the consultant develops an increasing clientele within the client company. By this time, the chief executive and the consultant have probably agreed upon a regular consulting day—once a week, once a month, or even less often—which the consultant is to spend at the client company. That day may be spent with more psychological studies and feedbacks but, if the consultant is to be maximally helpful, eventually the preponderance of time will be spent in other consulting activities.

A DAY AT SYSTEM CONTROLS COMPANY

At the beginning of a consulting day, Larry, the human resources director of System Controls Company, a medium-sized firm, called in the consulting psychologist. The following conversation took place.

Consultant: "How are things going?"

Larry: "Great, if you happen to like living in a pressure cooker! Which brings me to why I wanted to see you today. You know that stress management program you did for a group of us a couple of years ago? I was wondering if, with all the pressure everybody's under now, you could design something to help people cope a little better. You can cut the tension with a knife around here these days, you know, with everybody running around with no clear direction provided."

Consultant: "You're seeing a lot of wheel-spinning?"

Larry: "Sure. Everybody is running in place, waiting for the next shoe to drop, waiting for *him* to decide which way we're going to go, and *he* just keeps encouraging everybody."

Consultant: "You mean John?" (*John is the president.*)

Larry: "He is living on borrowed time. We've got our biggest competitor already coming out with a cheaper version of our M-240, and Research is 18 months behind on the enhancement that was supposed to protect us—and now they're wasting precious time trying to iron out the kinks they designed into the T-400 in the first place! So, the M-240, which is 40 percent of our sales dollars, is going down the tubes at the same time that we're bank-rolling Research's learning curve for a product that's projected to amount to only 5 percent of sales, *if* it's ever completed!"

Consultant: "So the M-240 people are feeling pretty demoralized?"

Larry: "Those who don't have their resumes already on the street are scared to death, and everybody's accusing each other and playing politics. So, I figured, we've got to do something to lower the tension around here or we are going to have a bunch of heart attack cases on our hands. Just the other day, Steve (*the sales director*) and Wynn (*the plant manager*) were having a screaming match because Wynn refuses to believe Steve's M-240 projections. He doesn't want to gear up to Steve's forecast, and then get caught with his pants down later, and have to lay off 200 people. Now, you know the kind of guy Steve is—he never gets ruffled.

But, he turned red and slammed his fist on the table, and I would've sworn that he was about to strangle Wynn. That's when I decided we needed to do something about the stress around here. We're never going to get anywhere if everybody is screaming at each other."

Consultant: "That must've been tough for you—seeing Steve blow up like that and realizing there was little you could do . . . then and there . . . to help out."

Larry: (shrugging) "It's been that way a lot lately—people coming to me with their troubles, and me being between a rock and a hard place—not wanting to knock John's leadership and not wanting to bad-mouth Research, on the one hand, and on the other hand, seeing what this is doing to everybody and listening to everybody's troubles."

Consultant: "So, for the time being, you're kind of stuck with everybody else's burdens on your shoulders."

Larry: "And the longer it goes, the worse it gets."

It is helpful to focus on this conversation between the human resources director and the consulting psychologist because it illuminates a number of ideas about the choices that the consultant needs to make and the ways in which the consultant plans his interventions. At first, we see that the consultant keeps things open-ended, avoids leading, and encourages further communication. Most important, he eases the conversation away from the client's proposed solution, the stress management seminar, so as to avoid falling into the trap of treating the symptom and ignoring the cause.

The psychologist is aware that two types of transactions are juxtaposed in this conversation. First, Larry is attempting to inform and to contract with an outside vendor on behalf of the organization. Yet, the psychologist gradually deemphasizes that component of the transaction, placing greater emphasis, instead, on a second element of the transaction, namely that between therapist and client.

Certainly there is much validity to the reality Larry describes, but in addition, Larry suggests a number of personally meaningful themes as he appears to be describing the situation outside of himself:

1. *"help people cope"* suggests a need to rescue others.

2. The emphatic use of the pronoun *"he"* for the president suggests anger at the imperfection of the authority figure, John.

3. *"no direction," "living on borrowed time,"* and *"was supposed to protect us"* suggest issues of vulnerability and helplessness under conditions of alarm (*"going down the tubes"*).

4. *"Steve never gets ruffled"* suggests some fear of emotionality or confrontation (*"politics"*).

5. *"I would have sworn he was about to strangle Wynn"* suggests that Larry unconsciously equates the expression of anger with violence.

The psychologist recalls Larry's psychological study: his violent, alcoholic father; his ambivalence toward authority figures; his paralyzing stoic overcontrol in the face of fear; and, his larger-than-life "peacemaker" script that he carried with him from his childhood, and which influenced his decision to go into human resources. These themes are woven into the fabric of his strengths and shortcomings, especially under stress. The consultant uses the word *"stuck"* ambiguously to echo Larry's externalized *"running in place."* With qualifications like *"then and there"* and *"for the time being,"* he seeds the implication that what is stuck can be unstuck, and that current feelings of helplessness can yield to feelings of empowerment.

At a psychodynamic level, the consultant's further work with Larry is fairly well cut out for him. The themes suggested by Larry's imagery fit with the impressions the psychologist derived at the time of the psychological study and, in fact, Larry himself had already evidenced some intellectual understanding of these themes and their day-to-day effects. In time, as Larry signals readiness, the consultant will continue to try to help him to come more to terms with these themes and to gain psychological distance, to triangulate in psychological space, to step outside of his habitual reactions in order to more effectively manage them.

Concurrently, the consultant will help Larry to explore various behavioral alternatives open to him in order for him to be more effective in his organizational role. Larry's condescending protection of John, the president, and his apparent reluctance to confront John directly; his failure to draw any *positive* energy from Steve's outburst; his nonconstructive siding with the M-240 people over those involved with the T-400 line; his implicit catastrophizing of his complainants' anguish, and his resultant failure to help them to hold themselves accountable for constructive action, are all issues that will likely be the focus of the rest of this meeting (and probably others). In all likelihood, these themes will provide the fabric into which the consultant will begin weaving those themes that are less conscious and less directly accessible.

Thus, the consultant has begun an opportunistic excursion with Larry, very much akin to the process of psychotherapy, though less formal, less scheduled, and more complex in the variety of agenda and the multiplicity of roles. The consultant will test and retest his hypotheses as he listens to, and tries to make sense of, Larry's experience of Larry, others' experience of Larry, as well as his own experience of Larry. As in psychotherapy, there is a disjointed quality to dealing with all of Larry's agenda, and the psychologist needs to have some kind of holistic vision within which to integrate his impressions about Larry. The consultant's excursion is opportunistic in that he ambles along in his relationship with Larry, looking for veins to mine or crevices within which to plant seeds. Within the cavernous environs of the therapeutic relationship, the consultant must be patient with darkness and ambiguity, skilled at detecting faint signs, and practiced at distinguishing between the surrounding sounds and his own inner voices.

The relationship with Larry is, then, a psychotherapeutic relationship. It lacks the distilled purity of the psychotherapist's office with its 50-minute-hour and once-a-week disciplines, as well as its sense of being away from the noisiness of one's daily activities. It is therapy "on the fly," and it lacks tranquility and elegance. On the other hand, this relationship offers the benefits of greater situational relevance and context as well as the call to action inherent in organizational life. The psychologist's role may be made more difficult by the increased complexity, but this same complexity widens his or her overall perspective of the individual. The person is seen, not in static isolation, but in dynamic interaction with relevant others. Each approach has its own costs and benefits, and the consultant may sometimes find it appropriate to suggest that a particular person follow up the consulting relationship with more formal psychotherapy in order to deal more systematically or directly with the intrapsychic issues.

J. Watson Wilson, one of the early consultants in the field, used to say that he was the envy of clinicians providing individual psychotherapy because he had the opportunity to actually be in the world of the individual client. Just as family therapists have the advantage of seeing the whole family unit in action, the management psychologist has the added advantage of actually observing, impacting upon, and cross-referencing the real world of the individual.

As the conversation with Larry continues, the consultant makes a number of mental notes about whom he should make sure to see on this or subsequent consulting visits. Paul, who reports to Steve (the sales director), has already asked to see him, and he wonders if Paul's request has anything to do with Steve's recent state of mind. In any case, he concludes, it would probably be wise to touch base with Paul first to become a little more acquainted with the lay of the land. As field support manager, perhaps Paul has been getting the heat about M-240 from the regional offices or perhaps he is having difficulty eliciting cooperation from his counterparts in Wynn's manufacturing operation. After meeting with Paul, he will probably need to decide the order in which to see John, Steve, Wynn, and Rudy (the research director) since each is likely to have a good deal on his mind.

The conversations are likely to begin with a, "How have things been going?", to be followed soon by the unfolding of yet another viewpoint about the crisis at hand. Each perspective will probably be mostly correct, but just enough askew to reflect scripted predispositions and too-narrow lines of sight. Each person is likely to identify one or more of the others as "the problem," and to be partially correct, except insofar as his own failure to step outside himself is limiting his possibilities. The psychologist will attempt to promote what some psychologists would call the development of an "observing ego," what Bier (1988) calls "arousal of uncertainty," and what Mangham (1978) calls "alienation," and defines as "the art of making the familiar strange by stepping outside it. It is the process of disrupting the taken-for-grantedness of everyday life."[1] This breaking of familiar sets can occur at a very conscious, situation-based level, or at the level of unconscious defenses whose purpose it is to stabilize certain core assumptions and misperceptions.

A CLINICAL VIEW OF CHANGE

Central to the clinical perspective in psychological consulting to management is the belief that here—in the habitual scripts, the core misperceptions, the unconscious defenses, and the individual's subjectivity and internal dialogue—is where change is most beguilingly resisted, at both an individual and organizational level. Certainly change can occur in the absence of an explicitly intrapsychic focus (see Ullmann & Krasner, 1966; Watzlawick, Weakland & Fisch, 1974), but in its complete absence the consultant risks walking blindly through a mine field of psychological resistances. It is this lack of attention to intrapsychic reality (or at least individual-to-individual reality) that leads clinicians to regard certain non-clinically trained consultants to industry as missing the *sine qua non,* and therefore as potentially naive and superficial in their nomothetic assessments and group interventions.

I once attended a conference led by some rather prominent non-clinically trained organizational consultants, and I was struck by the amount of hostility that was expressed toward particular individuals in their client companies who had managed to thwart their nobly conceived, group-oriented interventions. They seemed to be saying, in effect, that everything would go really well if only people and their personalities didn't keep getting in the way. Much of the strategy that was discussed regarding building client relationships involved going around difficult people and manipulating allegiances of "enlightened" organization members.

Certainly, consulting is very tough work, but when you begin without genuine respect for the individual and without a framework for understanding individuals at an individual level, you just make a tough job tougher. Tendencies toward error are magnified when the consultant approaches the people in organizations programmatically or faddishly, waving banners of complete openness and authenticity, unselfish cooperation, participative management, uniform sharing of values, or "enlightened" organizational "architecture." Such programmatic solutions may backfire because they fail to address the causes of problems that lie within individuals.

In 210 B.C., Petronius Arbiter[2] said:

> "We trained hard, but it seemed that every time we were beginning to form up into teams, we would be reorganized. I was to learn later in life that we tend to meet any new situation by reorganizing: and a wonderful method it can be for creating an illusion of progress while producing confusion, inefficiency, and demoralization!" (Quoted by Mangham [1978])

The clinical approach assumes that when people are organized "the wrong way," it is not because they do not have a consultant or a piece of academic research or a book on Japanese management styles to point them the right way. The clinician assumes that they have chosen to organize themselves the way they have because they are who they are. He or she assumes further that the "right" way to organize or to move forward will depend upon the characteristics of the individuals being organized. At least, that is where the search will begin. What the consultant *does* will depend upon what he or she hears and understands—not upon what is in the current tool box.

Similarly, in looking for ways to be helpful to Larry's organization, he will build his particular reality structure upon the foundation of individual personalities, and go from there. All sorts of group-oriented interventions suggest themselves in the short conversation with Larry. Perhaps the managers as a group need to work on their teamwork so that they may achieve greater consensus. Perhaps they need some work on strategic thinking and decision-making as they face a serious competitive threat. Perhaps they need to work on their openness with each other so that Rudy (in research) and John (the president) get more feedback as to how others view their priorities. It is possible that such group interventions may occur to the consultant; yet, they are not likely to be his starting point. They are likely to strike him, at least initially, as too simple, too easy, and too short-lived. He views change as something that requires deep and extensive roots to have fundamental and lasting value.

It may occur to the consultant that the organization is not well-structured to handle two divergent product lines, both of which are competing for valuable organizational resources. After all, systems have a way of teaching people how not to think and organizational structures tend to tell people with whom not to communicate and cooperate. Perhaps decentralization might be the organizational Draino that unplugs the M-240. This, too, he considers—in fact, it is probably suggested to him by a number of managers seeking autonomy as a way out of the mess. Yet, the consultant reserves his judgment for now, waiting instead for all the pieces to fall into place (see Levinson, 1972).

Nor is he likely to agree—for now—to the requested stress management program, even though he does a real fine one and even though people *are* experiencing stress. He is concerned that an agreement to do such a program would distract the organization from its real issues and would embed him in the very system of wheel-spinning from which he is attempting to help the organization emerge. Since much of what executives do is manage uncertainty, they often grapple with the feelings of vulnerability with which uncertainty and ambiguity are associated. It is at such times that impatience with the darkness leads people to look "where the light is better," rather than where the problems are. A strength of the clinical approach lies in its emphasis on clarifying questions and resisting answers. The consultant must be careful not to add confirmation to the organization's illusions by participating in them. As Weinberg (1985) has said, "It may look like a crisis, but it's only the end of an illusion."[3]

Paradoxically, as Haley (1984) has observed, often "ordeals" or rituals that may have little obvious relationship to the problems they are designed to cure can be of value in that they unfreeze people. Therefore, the consultant must maintain a certain flexibility and iconoclasm with respect to his or her own world view and preferred intervention strategy. There is, in fact, a place for superficiality, and as the behavior therapists have shown, sometimes treating the symptom removes the problem (see Ullmann and Krasner, 1966, pp 1–63). Sometimes, it is necessary to give what the client asks for, if it is reasonably sound, in order to establish the credibility required to later not give what is asked for, but rather what is needed.

The danger is in using this reasoning consistently as a convenient excuse. At the very minimum, there is a certain responsibility to the client to express loudly, repeatedly, and in no uncertain terms the reservation that treating the symptom could provide false comfort, and that any attempt to do so must be accompanied by a plan to address root causes. If the consultant can take anything for granted, one assumption would be that people look too much to short-term fixes and bandaids and too little to long-term efforts. Just as psychotherapy aims to help a person increase his or her level of maturity, the clinical approach to organizational consulting attempts to help organizations make day-to-day decisions that are truly aligned with the organization's long-term interests.

Accordingly, in addressing Larry's current frustrations, and those that are likely to become evident with others as the issue of M-240 and T-400 plays itself out, the consultant will have to make choices as to whether to intervene for the sake of the short run or the long run. The consultant will have to choose between interventions that have immediate, practical results and those that may sacrifice immediate gain for the eventual growth and development of the individuals, thereby contributing to the ultimate strength of the organization in the long run. For example, he may offer Larry a well-grounded interpretation of his behavior and advice as to how he might reach out and be helpful to John. But, if the consultant does so, he risks creating dependency and losing a chance to help Larry more deeply explore some of his issues. On the other hand, if he is too indirect, too idealistic perhaps, he risks losing an opportunity to help Larry and the organization deal with an important crisis, and he further risks having no impact in the long run at all. These are the judgment calls the consultant must make, and the only guiding rule I know is to realize in doing whatever one does, that one has also chosen *not* to do the something else.

In a similar vein, in helping managers decide how to manage their subordinates, the consultant often has the opportunity to illuminate the same dilemma between short-term gain and long-term growth. For example, the manager may choose to rescue a subordinate from a failing project by "helping" but, in so doing, prevent the subordinate from learning much more profound lessons. For both the manager and the consultant it is often all too easy to let present problems dictate solutions and to forget the ultimate goal of empowerment.

As the psychologist "does his rounds," he encounters various people wrestling with their own pieces of the puzzle into which Larry's perspective gives us a glimpse, but he is not particularly likely to decide for himself what the "right" solution should be. Even if he did, it would be gratuitous for him to express his opinion. Instead, it is his role to help the individuals clarify their options and make choices with greater objectivity, less automaticity, and with greater consideration for ultimate effects.

At times, he will serve as an interpreter, helping the various individuals to understand the divergent realities that might otherwise lead to incomprehension, suspicion, distrust, and name-calling. The consultant's role as interpreter of linguistic and nonverbal meaning is identical to the one the therapist may play in the context of marriage counseling. It is likely, for example, that Steve's outburst toward Wynn was not simply a function of Steve's disagreement with Wynn, but of his understanding of Wynn's motives. Steve is likely to be so convinced of his own position that he views Wynn's disagreement with deep suspicion and considers Wynn's position to be "self-serving," "politicking," "butt-saving," rigid, ignorant, or evidence of Wynn's being a poor team player. The consultant, therefore, expects that in his discussions with Steve he may need to help Steve relegitimize Wynn and his ideas so that Steve can move from a position of nonconstructive contempt to one more likely to help Steve achieve his goals. He may well need to do the same with Wynn. The consultant also knows that Steve's self-inhibiting fear of failure had led him to limit his own capacity to creatively and effectively manage relations with research, to "pump up" a scared sales force, and to get Wynn to believe his figures. He may choose the occasion to help Steve sort out some of these issues.

The consultant may find that his expectations are not proven out—that what was psychologically meaningful to Larry meant much less to Wynn or Steve—so he needs to avoid fixing his preconceptions by holding them fluidly in reserve. He must juggle a number of contradictory hypotheses in the air until his instincts, his experience, and the preponderance of data tell him what's what. Because the M-240—T-400 issue is apparently so significant, the likelihood is that the consultant will spend many hours during the course of the current consulting day and subsequent consulting days dealing with that particular issue. In his contacts with people who are only peripherally involved, his question, "How are things going?" is likely to yield answers that will apprise him of the pervasiveness of the issue, and that will round out his own perception of what is really going on.

Concurrently, the consultant is likely to be dealing with a number of other issues that have arisen on past consulting visits and that will continue to arise during each visit. There is a discussion with Rudy, the research director, who has been trying to find a way to upgrade the quality of people in his organization by looking outside for potential hires or by developing the talents from within. Andrea, one of the regional sales managers, wants to consult about a salesperson whose sales are down and who may be showing signs of alcoholism. Ellie, the materials manager, wants to discuss her frustration with the performance review she just received from Wynn, in which Wynn described her as more of a technician than a broad "people manager." The psychologist follows up with Janet, the customer service manager, to see if the positive effects of their recent efforts at improving customer service have been maintained (the consultant had done a seminar with her group, focusing on issues of communication and self-accountability). Dan, the applications engineering manager, wishes to discuss a possible change in his organizational structure in order to accommodate the increasingly important role of the T-400 line. Dan is thinking of creating a position to be responsible solely for the T-400, and wants to discuss whether such a change makes sense and, if so, which of his subordinates would be best suited to managing that function.

John, the president, felt the deep loneliness and insecurity of making the critical choices about the M-240 and T-400 in the absence of good data or significant social support. To inspire the others (and to reassure himself), he felt he needed to maintain a very positive tone. Yet, his failure to express his doubts led his staff to wonder if he were wearing rose-colored glasses. John is frustrated because he sees Steve as giving up on the M-240 in the face of the present difficulties, rather than finding creative solutions for dealing with the competitive threat. He wants to help Steve feel more empowered to be creative as well as to more effectively negotiate with the research department for M-240 time. John is concerned and angry about Research's inability to focus on two lines at once, and wonders to the consultant if Rudy has what it will take to make things happen. He is also frustrated at his own boss, the group president, who is reluctant to put more money into the research effort, and at his own failure to be more persuasive with his own boss. He sees Larry as a "cry baby," and asks the consultant's advice so as to help Larry play a more constructive role. He questions his own leadership style and asks the consultant for help in getting the group back to working as a team.

Jim, the manager of engineering design, contacts the consultant about the stress he is under because he feels the impossible is being asked of him and his engineers as they are grappling with M-240 and T-400. His group is getting pressure from its boss, Rudy, the research director, from the planning people who are pushing for earlier dates, from the manufacturing people who say the designs are impractical, and from John himself, who scowls every time he comes near the engineering department.

Each new contact provides new leads for the consultant, new opportunities to strike while the iron is hot, where a crisis may be brewing, where someone may be ready to grow. The consultant takes the initiative of contacting people and inserting himself into situations where he thinks he can be of greatest benefit, rather than passively waiting for clients to call. To do so well the consultant must always be opportunistically poised and must not be so confined to particular programs or techniques that his options are reduced. It takes a good deal of resourcefulness, but offers a great deal of excitement as well as the reward of impacting when and where constructive influence is needed.

---

1. From *Interactions and interventions in organizations,* by I. M. Mangham, copyright © 1978 by John Wiley & Sons, Inc. Reprinted by permission of the publisher.

2. Quoted in *Interactions and interventions in organizations,* by I. M. Mangham, copyright © 1978 by John Wiley & Sons, Inc. Reprinted by permission of the publisher.

3. From *The secrets of consulting: A guide to giving & getting advice successfully,* by G. M. Weinberg, copyright © 1985 by Dorset House Publishing. Reprinted by permission of the publisher.

7

Challenges to Objectivity

*Untruthfulness and dishonesty were with me, as with most people,
called into being in so immediate, so contingent a fashion, and in
self-defense, by some particular interest, that my mind, fixed on
some lofty ideal, allowed my character, in the darkness below, to
set about those urgent, sordid tasks, and did not look down to
observe them.*

Marcel Proust (*The Guermantes Way*)

In consulting, the frequency with which one question is
asked often defines the clinical approach: Whose needs are
being met—the client's or the consultant's? Psychological
consulting to management is a world where things count—
where your ego, your impact, your acceptance and, ultimately,
your livelihood are affected by what you do and how you do it.
The prospect of being consciously or unconsciously self-
serving, at least sometimes, is an inevitability against which
constant internal vigilance is an essential safeguard. Inner
scrutiny is not the exclusive province of clinicians, but more
than in any other profession I know of, it is part of the
language, training, and practice of psychotherapists. More-
over, psychotherapists tend to think in terms of hidden
motives, so they have a conceptual framework within which
to place the data they collect. Psychotherapists do not have
an edge over others in maturity or in basic personal integrity,
but they do tend to cultivate an awareness of the kinds of
personal barriers to objectivity that can get in the way of a
change agent, and subtly skew results. As Anatole France said:

The faculty of doubting is rare among men. A few choice
spirits carry the germ of it in them, but these do not
develop without training. (*Penguin Island*)

63

In this chapter, I would like to share some examples with you where consulting mistakes were made because the consultant responded to his or her own needs rather than to those of the client. Some are mine and those of my colleagues; others I've encountered along the way.

BRAGGING

Charlie was providing feedback to Becky on the psychological study that Charlie did when Becky applied for a job with the Charlotte Manufacturing Company. During the course of the feedback, Charlie asked Becky how things had been going during the two months she had been on the job. Becky said she was very pleased. In particular, she liked the way managers were given a great deal of latitude within Charlotte's very decentralized structure. She stated that with her former employer she had felt much more restricted and had sometimes come into conflict as a result of "politics and bureaucracy." Charlie responded, "Yes, but believe it or not, Charlotte used to be that way until 11 years ago, when Noah Jacobs, the president who retired two years ago, made some significant changes around here. He and I figured that a great deal of wasted effort was going toward circumventing arbitrary organizational barriers instead of increasing productivity, so we invented the matrix management system you've been talking about."

Charlie's mention of his collaboration with the former president was wrong on three counts. First, it was bragging and, thus, contaminates the consultant's image. Second, the attention was drawn away from the client, Becky, and her needs. It may be, for example, that the issues of politics and bureaucracy which she found in her former organization were as much a function of her own tendencies and distortions as they were objective characterizations of the organization. The consultant lost the opportunity to probe this area and possibly to be of service. Third, the consultant has aligned himself with the power structure of the company. To Becky he will no longer be just a helpful consultant, but someone who has to be handled and reacted to in light of the authority structure at the company. Given what he has said, Charlie should not later be surprised when he is accused of making all the hiring and firing decisions for the company. People will be less likely to confide in Charlie and, eventually, the consulting relationship will be questioned because it will be felt that the consultant wields too much power and influence for an outsider.

Clients are vigilant with regard to well-meaning outsiders who do not distinctly define their own boundaries. The synapses between people and organizations are so sensitive that the entry into the system by the outsider is immediately felt and immediately leads to vigilance. The consultant must remove his or her own ego from the situation or trust will erode. Accepting credit for anything that happens in an organization is usually unwise because it implies illegitimate power on the part of the consultant, fosters the perception of organizational dependency on the consultant, and detracts from the organization's own sense of empowerment. More-over, the consultant is only accountable for his or her consulting—it is the individual in the organization who is accountable for the organizational action. It is presumptuous of Charlie to leap from the reality of his deep involvement with the former president to joining with the president's accounta-bility for the actions taken with the words "we invented."

Consulting is lonely work. Charlie worked alone and had little opportunity to "brag" to peers. Here was an organization to which he had contributed much. Yet, with the departure of the former president, he had lost the one person who could most appreciate his value. In trying to fill the void, he damaged his own credibility as a consultant, thus eroding the very relationship that had sustained him. Sadly, this process can lead to vicious circles, wherein a consultant deals with the erosion of a relationship by filling the voids the erosion creates at the expense of the relationship itself. This process can be most insidious when it is not recognized by the consultant, as may be the case when a major change takes place in a client organization that leads to a sense of loss but no direct immediate change in the consulting contract. In the above example, Charlie had insufficiently held up to his own light his sense of loss when the former president left the company.

OVERIDENTIFICATION WITH THE UNDERDOG

Julia was consulting with two key vice presidents of Valerie Mutual, an insurance company. They felt extreme pressure from the new president, George, to take certain swift actions to make the company more entrepreneurial and aggressive. George complained that the vice presidents were too slow, too cautious, too conservative, and too set in their ways, and he had threatened both of them with firing if they did not move ahead. As Julia consulted with the vice presidents, she sensed their almost panicky response to George's call to action. They were asking her for help about what to do in response to George's "impossible" demands. The thrust of Julia's response was that the vice presidents should calm down, slow down, and proceed with caution. She counseled working on their communication with George, in order to better understand "where he was coming from," and to be better able to respond. Yet, this was exactly the kind of response George was threatening to fire them for.

Julia had fallen into the trap of overidentifying with the panicky reactions of the vice presidents in the face of George's call to action. Julia, herself, was a peaceful, somewhat restrictive type of person who was ruffled by emotional chaos. She saw the vice presidents responding *unnaturally,* as it was uncharacteristic of them to be proactive and because they were afraid to be so. Instead of accepting the *unnaturalness* of their behavior as the first false starts toward growth, she hooked right into the vice presidents' own fears that mobilization would lead to disruption and chaos. Rather than helping them to deal with their fears of change, she reified them. Additionally, she got trapped into defining the problem the way it was posed by the client. They had asked her what to do, and she so identified with them and their consternation, that she neglected to realize that there was no reason why she should have any idea what they should do. If they were to live up to their titles as vice presidents, *they* would have to figure out what needed to be done and take the actions to do it. A more appropriate role for Julia would have been to help them see the opportunity in the crisis.

FAILING TO TRUST ONE'S GUT

Lauren did a psychological evaluation with a candidate for Vice President of Manufacturing at Vaughn Engineering. The candidate was brilliant, articulate, and able to provide sound answers to all the questions that Lauren asked. The test results and comprehensive interview findings confirmed a pattern of solid emotional health and substantial career growth. Yet, Lauren simply did not trust the candidate. Something in her gut said he was lying and that he was probably psychopathic. Lauren dutifully presented all the data to a colleague, Karen, and the two of them reanalyzed it thoroughly. Nothing, they concluded, pointed to psychopathy. Perhaps, it was Lauren's own issues of counterexploitiveness that had surfaced, they conjectured. So Lauren wrote up the psychological study in accordance with the data and presented it to management. Fortunately, the personnel manager had done a little tracking of her own, and had found a long path in the candidate's past of alcoholism, underhandedness, and firings.

Lauren had succumbed and overrode her gut reaction because all the data pointed against it. When she and Karen reanalyzed the data, there was, of course, no reason to expect that Karen would find anything in the data that she, herself, had not already found. What Karen lacked, since she had not met the candidate personally, was the one critical piece of Lauren's data—her gut reaction—that made all the difference. In part, Lauren's mistake occurred because she had put the pressure on herself to come up with a definitive answer for her client. Somehow it seemed wrong to charge the client for the evaluation and to give an answer like, "My head says X but my gut says Y, so you'd better do a better reference check." Yet, that would have been precisely the best answer she could have given.

STUMBLING INTO RESISTANCE

Tony was referred to Acme Fabrications by its bank. Acme was being forced to reorganize under Chapter 11 Bankruptcy, and the psychologist was called in to help senior managers plan an effective strategy for paring down the existing organization and creating a new, more viable organization for the future. Acme had been highly leveraged and was hit simultaneously by a major recession, a major cutback in spending by its customers, unfavorable international currency exchange trends, and the introduction of two new products by different competitors that were both superior to two similar products offered by Acme. The eight senior managers had a week to design and implement an effective reorganization strategy. If such a strategy were not forthcoming within the specified time, the bankruptcy court promised the creditors that an outside transitional team would be appointed to assume management control of Acme. It was clear to everyone that about 65 percent of the company's operations would have to liquidated, and about 65 percent of its people would have to be fired with minimal severance benefits.

Tony realized that there was a significant opportunity in the present crisis to create a new organization out of the ashes of the old one that would be able to thrive and to meet future challenges. The existing senior managers could pool their deep understanding of the business in order to make the critical decisions regarding which divisions would be saved and which ones liquidated. In addition, they had a unique opportunity to select the strongest people to serve the new organization and, thus, to retain for the new organization a wealth of human capital that the old organization had taken years to build. Tony and the senior managers at Acme knew well that a court-appointed transition team would have neither the inclination nor the penetrating understanding to perform such delicate surgery. Nor would it be very likely to seek the advice of a team whose apparent failure it was being called in to rectify. Rather, the team would probably use a meat cleaver to somewhat arbitrarily chop off unprofitable operations. Its focus would likely be on cutting current negative cash flow, with much less emphasis on designing future vigor into the surviving entity. The senior managers and Tony needed to work against time.

The group worked hard and around the clock. Tony pressed his emphasis on the opportunity within the present crisis. He tried to help them articulate and communicate about various strategies, and to envision the ways the new organization would have to be staffed in order to best tap the available human resources. Naturally, these discussions engendered discomfort, since each scheme necessitated the departure of some of the key managers taking part in the discussions. As the clock continued to run down, it became clear that the group could not reach a consensus. The participants vehemently disagreed over the current assets and liabilities—financial, market, and human—of each of the company's current operations. Therefore, they found it impossible to agree on the very fundamental assumptions regarding organizational strengths and weaknesses that they, as insiders, could use to create an organization that was better positioned to confront the future than one that would be created by an external transition team. Despite the best of intentions, Tony's valiant efforts failed to unite them toward dealing constructively from common purposes.

One reason Tony failed was that, in fact, their purposes were not common. Each manager realized only too well that the odds were only about 50/50 that his or her services would be required by the new organization. Without even the hope of a "golden parachute" they had to think about serious cash-flow problems of their own. In Maslow's terms, they were operating at the safety or security level, and were, therefore, unable to reach out toward greater purposes, despite their conscious intents to do so. In fact, their sincere expressed intentions helped to fool Tony into thinking that progress could be made. He tended to dismiss the heated arguments as being the result of all the tension the people were under, and he forgot that the arguments were also a clue as to the level of constructiveness that could be expected. Tony was so absorbed in the challenge of creating the new organization that he failed to adequately take the pulse of the leaders of the old one. He forgot that he was the only one in the room who had little to lose from any reorganization and, therefore, he failed to attend sufficiently to the possibility that high personal stakes would interfere with the managers' ability to remain objective. Certainly, he acknowledged these possibilities, but he took at face value the group members' assertions that they had the "maturity" to look beyond their own interests.

It is far from clear that *any* approach would have worked, given the lack of common purposes and the distractions caused by personal fears of losing one's job. It can be concluded, however, that for an approach to have worked, it would have had to have taken personal concerns into greater account. It might have been helpful for some guarantee to have been made to provide a future job or a "golden parachute" for each of the senior managers; however, it would be very unlikely for a bankruptcy court to agree to such terms. Furthermore, such a self-serving gesture on the part of senior management would not bode well for establishing cohesiveness among the rest of the surviving employees. With no simple solutions, it would seem that Tony would have been more helpful had he spent more time working with the group in ways that more directly and meaningfully addressed each individual's personal agenda. For this group to have been able to move forward, it would have had to better deal with the issues of personal insecurity, familial obligation, guilt over betraying loyal subordinates, and the like.

ALLOWING MIXED AGENDA TO SURFACE

Mark was consulting with Eileen, the president of Donald Industries, about Donald's efforts to acquire a small company in a small town in another part of the country. Eileen was discussing her frustration in dealing with the hard bargaining of the sellers as well as their obvious enormous ambivalence about selling the company they had founded. One of the questions at hand was whether Eileen could trust the sellers to follow through on their commitment to stay involved and share their expertise for three years. Mark helped Eileen to explore the motivations of the individual sellers. They discussed the ways Eileen might best approach the negotiations, as well as how to frame the final contract to ensure compliance. After a fairly lengthy conversation, Eileen's assistant served coffee. During the pause in the conversation, Mark asked, "Which airport do you use to get there?"

Eileen knew exactly why Mark had asked the question. If the acquisition were successfully completed, Mark would be likely to gain a new consulting client from the process. His question was irrelevant and, more important, it took the focus off Eileen's issues and put it onto Mark's self-serving agenda. Worst of all, the two had just been discussing Eileen's frustrations in trying to trust people with mixed agenda! Eileen was opening up to Mark because she needed someone with no ax to grind, and Mark responded by putting his ax right on the table.

SHOWING OFF ONE'S WIT

Colleen was consulting with Jeffrey, the owner and president of Bob's Mart, a regional supermarket chain. Jeffrey was also the president of his synagogue, where there had been much turmoil of late. A number of parents had repeatedly failed to pay the Hebrew school tuitions of their children, and the new principal of the Hebrew school reacted one day by sending those children home. Jeffrey wanted to discuss the behavior of the principal with Colleen and said, "You don't think that was the right thing to do, do you?" Colleen, seeing the opportunity for humor, responded, "It certainly wasn't the Christian thing to do." The two of them laughed at Colleen's joke and then continued their discussion about the situation at the synagogue.

Jeffrey understood the humor in Colleen's joke and also knew that no prejudice was involved. Yet, at some level, her joke had to be processed and "forgiven." For the first time in their consulting relationship, Colleen had made her non-Jewishness an issue. Never again did Jeffrey mention anything having to do with his temple or with Jewishness to Colleen, and Colleen tells me she is convinced that Jeffrey is not even consciously aware of this subtle change in their relationship.

TAKING ON "THE OLD MAN"

Jason, the owner and president of J. B. Fredda, a small manufacturing company, wanted to bring his son, Brad, into the business in order to groom him for taking over the business upon Jason's retirement. Jason's lawyer referred him to Nick, the consultant, in order to get an objective outsider's viewpoint about Brad's capabilities. As the consultant and Jason talked about Brad, it became clear to Nick that Jason was not facing up to the serious implications of some obvious immaturities and weaknesses in his son. Nick surmised that this was the reason for the lawyer's referral—that Jason had made up his mind to bring his son on board, notwithstanding his lawyer's advice to the contrary. The lawyer was hoping, Nick concluded, that a psychological evaluation of Brad would drive home to Jason the folly of bringing him into the firm. Nick did the evaluation and pointed out to Brad and to Jason all the reasons why Brad would be a poor fit. Jason brought Brad into the firm and terminated the consulting relationship with Nick.

On the surface, Nick did a courageous thing, since he foresaw the strong likelihood that Jason would "kill the messenger." On the other hand, Nick accomplished little with all his courage. Nick had felt impatient with Jason's outrageous blindness in viewing his son. Unconsciously, Nick was reacting to his own father's favoritism of his older brother, and he was doing so with the same ploy he used against his own father, namely taking on "the old man" to show him "how dumb he really is." As with his father, Nick won the battle and lost the war, as the scenario played itself out with the inevitability of a Greek tragedy.

Since Jason's rejection of a negative evaluation of Brad was very likely, Nick would have done better not to do one. Instead, he could have tried to help Jason clarify his worries, fears, and feelings of guilt regarding Brad, so that Jason could consciously deal with these issues in the open. Nick would then have been in a better position to help Jason most effectively manage Brad, and Jason would have been more prepared to deal with such issues. Furthermore, Nick could have started his relationship with Brad on a strictly developmental note and then perhaps have had a greater chance of reaching him.

NOT MANAGING ONE'S JOINING

Marie, the president and owner of Creations de Jeanne, a specialty products company, had been working with Penny, the consultant, on a variety of pressing strategic and personnel issues. Through many lengthy discussions, they had finally concluded that a number of simple, but painful, actions had to be taken in order to stop what was becoming a serious decline in profitability and morale. The people in the organization were complaining bitterly to Penny about Marie and her indecisiveness. A number of people had quit or were thinking about leaving. A number of programs—some of which Penny had been involved in fostering—were floundering and on the verge of collapse. Marie's feelings of inadequacy as a manager were leading her to tighten up and stand still. Penny had sounded numerous alarms in order to make Marie aware of the consequences of her inaction, but Marie, nevertheless, was still stuck.

During one of their conversations, Penny decided to "go for broke" to make her point: "Don't you realize that a lot of people are counting on you?" Penny asked. "That you have been complaining about these problems but not taking action? You have a lot of responsibility, and you really need to act now!" Marie responded, "I think you're working on the wrong problems. I don't know where you're coming from."

Penny's impatience with Marie only served to deepen Marie's insecurity and indecision. Penny felt like Marie's partner, helping to captain a ship in rough seas. Penny felt that they could sink any minute and felt let down because Marie was not doing her part. Penny's father had divorced her mother, a fearful, weak, and insecure woman who then relied on Penny to be the adult in the family. Penny had an enormous

ıcity to join in partnership with others, but she had great
ıculty defining the boundaries, so that she could appropri-
aṭly manage her joining. As with her mother, she had joined
into rather than joining *with* when she lectured Marie on
managing what was, after all, Marie's own company.

BEING A SERVANT OF POWER

Lynne, the Human Resources Manager of the Neppo
Corporation, a major capital equipment company, called up
Joel, the consultant, and asked if he did psychological
evaluations of executives. Joel indicated that he did and
agreed to meet with Lynne at her office one week later. At that
meeting, Lynne indicated that she needed help identifying
managerial talent in a group of supervisors and technical
employees. Lynne explained that there had been poor morale
in the company in recent years, because many employees had
the perception that, in order to get ahead at Neppo, one had to
have the right connections or had to play political games.
Promotions were seen as based on favoritism. Worse yet,
there was a feeling that upper management had little regard
for most of the employees and, therefore, mostly looked outside the company for key positions rather than developing
and promoting people from within. A recent attitude survey
that Lynne had done had confirmed the worst: the employees
felt deeply disrespected by management and were, in turn,
deeply distrustful of management.

As one way of addressing these concerns, Lynne had persuaded the key senior managers to budget for a management
development training program. The program was to be run on
company time, but employees would be required to do homework assignments on their own time. As Lynne explained it,
the program was intended to be a way of saying that the
company would indeed support an employee's growth as long
as that employee was willing to bear some of the responsibility. The program was advertised among 960 technical and
supervisory workers. The response astounded Lynne and the
key managers: Instead of the roughly 5 percent response they
expected, 367 employees signed up for the program. Lynne

explained that there was no way the company could afford the expense and lost time for such a large group. She, therefore, wanted to narrow the group down to a more manageable 40 or 50 top candidates, based on their genuine promotability. In other words, the company wanted to put its educational investment where it was most likely to pay off.

Joel indicated that it would be cost-prohibitive to try to do a full psychological study with each of the 367 applicants. He suggested, instead, that a series of paper and pencil tests be administered to each applicant. One test would be a widely validated test of intelligence. The second would be a widely used measure of managerial motivation. Joel indicated that he could rank the candidates based on their performance on the two tests. Since this procedure was fairly inexact, he suggested that a more ideal solution would be for him to personally interview the top 70 or 80 applicants, and add his clinical judgment into the equation. Lynne indicated that the cost of Joel's time for interviewing would be prohibitive so they agreed on testing only. When the program was announced, only 26 people signed up for testing. Management interpreted this as a sign that the majority of people were not really interested in the program in the first place. The plan to use psychological tests was abandoned, since voluntary attrition achieved the result for which the tests where intended. During the course of the next year the rate of turnover among technical and supervisory personnel increased sharply and morale declined even further. Joel never did establish a consulting relationship with Neppo.

Joel was so eager to please, so enticed by Neppo, and so easily caught up in the problem the way the client defined it, that he failed to see that Lynne and the management of Neppo were using him in a way that would camouflage their betrayal of their own employees. Senior management was once again manifesting disrespect and engendering distrust by going back on the promise of management development for all who requested it. Perhaps they were unaware of this and rationalized that what they were doing was a step in the right direction. Yet, they were failing to see the degree to which they were only perpetuating the climate of distrust. Instead of agreeing to become a quasi-legitimate "executioner" for management, Joel would have better spent his time helping the senior managers to explore the real reasons for employee dissatisfaction, and how their own behavior may have made matters worse. This was Joel's worst mistake.

Joel's next error, which is very common, was the way he proposed to use psychological tests. There has never been and likely never will be a test of managerial motivation that predicts more than a small amount of managerial behavior. This is a matter of statistical reality, empirical reality, and psychological reality (see Hogan & Nicholson, 1988; Kagan, 1988; Kenrick & Funder, 1988; Mischel, 1968; Meehl, 1978; Wiggins, 1973). Furthermore, whatever the initial predictive value a test has, that value decreases as the population to which it is applied becomes more homogeneous, such as the group with which Lynne was concerned. Similarly, to the extent that the criterion for managerial effectiveness differs in the current population from the validity population, the value of the test as a predictor diminishes. Moreover, the majority of managerial tests do not meet minimal requirements for validity and, if they do, their generalizability is questionable.

Actuarial predictions, even when appropriately validated, require a willingness to live with the consequences of false negatives and false positives. The lower the variance accounted for by a test, the greater the percentage such misses will be. There are significant problems with employers' use of such tests with current employees; employers owe their current employees more than blind actuarial objectivity, unless it is proven beyond doubt that the actuarial approach surpasses any other approach or combination of approaches in reducing the number of misses. Seldom do organizations accept this burden of proof. When psychologists allow themselves to be associated with this mixture of scientistic naivete and actuarial zealousness, they unwittingly participate in the dehumanization of the workplace. Although a statistically forced mistake (e.g., a false negative) about an outside candidate applying for a job may be regrettably acceptable, it is unacceptable to make such a mistake about a member of one's own corporate family—and it is unnecessary.

USING A SLEDGEHAMMER

Diane was expressing her frustration to Jill, the consultant: "Ever since the reorganization, there has been a power play between Connie and Beverly and their departments. Even though Beverly is supposed to be reporting to Connie, nobody believes that that's the whole story. Connie is trying a power play and it is very demoralizing to everybody in Beverly's department, especially because they think that they are going to get caught in the power play." Jill had participated in the discussions that resulted in the decision to have Beverly and her department report to Connie. (Jill knew that, as far as upper management was concerned, there was no power play, but a decision to *reduce* ambiguity by consolidating the two departments.) Jill saw Diane as unintentionally contributing to her own frustration by not fully appreciating the clarity and finality of Connie's promotion. She wanted to alert Diane to the reality of the situation so that Diane would not trip over her own misperceptions. She realized that it would be important for Diane to behave in accordance with Connie's wishes, and that Diane would be perceived as being divisive if she maintained loyalty to Beverly at Connie's expense. Therefore, Jill said, "Diane, I think you're missing the point. There is no power struggle. Connie is in charge and that's that, but I see you not accepting that fact, even though the issue has already been decided."

The result of this conversation was that Diane spread the word among Beverly's supporters that Jill was on Connie's side. As a result, Jill was unable to help those individuals, including Diane, to sort out their various issues surrounding the organizational change.

Jill had used her understanding of the political reality as a hammer with which to "knock sense" into Diane. Yet, Diane had already shown her that she was resistant to accepting the reality of Connie's promotion. A more evocative approach with Diane would have been to help her explore constructive alternatives, which would have been less likely to have aroused Diane's resistance. Jill's heavy-handedness, though completely well-intended, called her objectivity into question with the very people in Beverly's department whom she was trying to help. Jill had been invested in the decision to consolidate departments. She had offered the consolidation as a solution to the departmental conflict that had been occurring and now she was impatient to see the hoped for cooperation and harmony. By pressing too fast for it, she delayed it.

WHISPERING "WOLF!"

David, the psychologist, had done psychological studies with all of the people who reported directly to Art, the vice president of finance of a medium-sized company. David had found that Art's subordinates were all rather hard-working and loyal but, unfortunately, none was higher than average in intelligence. David pointed out that their intellectual limitations would prevent them from dealing most effectively with conceptual issues. He pointed out that there was a particular danger to Art, since Art was not inclined to deal rigorously with detail. Art responded that, in the future, he would make a more concerted attempt to hire brighter people.

Two years later, Art discovered that the company's inventory had been overestimated by more than $2 million. This had occurred gradually over an 18-month period and was primarily the result of changes in the manufacturing systems that provided data to the finance department. Since the $2 million in inventory would have to be immediately written off the books, the company had to retract earlier statements to the financial press regarding expected profits. The result was a precipitous decline in the price of the company's stock as well as in the company's credibility with the Wall Street analysts. Art was forced to resign since, ultimately, it was his department's responsibility not to lose financial control.

It is difficult to fault David in this instance. After all, he had predicted exactly what had happened, namely that Art, because of his lack of detail orientation, would fail to catch the serious mistakes of which his subordinates were capable. On the other hand, David did not make his point compellingly. He had registered his point, but he had not made it register with

Art. In fact, David was never sure that his observations would turn out to have been important. He could not specify the exact way in which the problems would manifest themselves and, as a result, soft-peddled his own prediction that problems would manifest themselves. David's difficulty was heightened by the fact that Art had seen no current problems in the departments of any of his subordinates. Thus, David felt on very thin ground in making his fateful prediction. Yet, if the prediction was worth making at all, it was worth making clearly and compellingly not only in terms of the future but also in terms of the current situation. That is, if David's prediction was valid for the future, it could probably have also been validated at the time it was made. Had David really believed in his own prediction, he could have challenged Art to look deeply into his present organization in order to seek out those gaps that were not then being conceptually bridged. Even in the absence of such current validation, David could have much more strongly pressed his case, helping Art to save his job and helping the company to avoid an uncomfortable period.

Often, the consultant makes predictions in psychological space without the benefit of real-world coordinates. The consultant may be unable to concretize because of insufficient data, overly abstract thinking, or the fear of excluding possibilities. At such times, it may be helpful for the consultant to coax *the manager* into doing the concretizing. For example, David might have said to Art, "You've got to help me here. I know something very serious could go wrong in your department, but you'll have to help me figure out what that could be."

NAME-CALLING

Nat was invited by the Berlyn Lampshade Company to run a seminar on management styles for 30 senior managers from around the country who were attending Berlyn's annual senior management meeting. Nat had all the managers take a widely used test that divided managers among four quadrants which purported to describe major management styles:

"dominant," "analytical," "conservative," and "social." At one point in his highly entertaining lecture, Nat asked, "Who are the four who fell into the dominant quadrant?" As the four managers raised their hands, Nat said, "Aha, there are the Nazis!"

Nat's comment was intended to help the four managers recognize the adverse side of their styles. However, there were three unintended consequences of Nat's remark—one obvious, and two less obvious. First, Nat's label stuck. From that day on, many comments were made, mostly behind the back, about the four "Nazis." Instead of teaching tolerance, Nat had provided a medium for intolerance. He had stereotyped the managers, and his expertise lent a stamp of authenticity to the stereotype. In fact, a number of managers at Berlyn, who were rather passive and averse to change, had already resented the aggressive styles of the four "dominant" managers. Nat did talk about the positive as well as the negative sides of the "dominant" style, but his use of the powerful epithet "Nazis" only served to highlight the negative.

Second, Nat's comment made a powerful statement about himself. His willingness to cavalierly label individuals so harshly—and in front of their peers—signaled a certain untrustworthiness, a lack of humanitarian compassion, and a judgmental attitude. Derisive humor may seed future after-dinner speeches, but it does not seed a trusting consulting relationship.

Last, it is questionable if Nat advanced the cause of management or of psychology by teaching that people could be put into one of four "nice little boxes." Such schema can sometimes be used to make the point that there is an upside and a downside to every style and also to stimulate people to look at themselves and at others. Yet, the major lesson that managers actually seem to learn from such exercises is that people *do* fit into nice little boxes. There is a fine line between simplifying and trivializing. In these days of one-minute books on interpersonal relations and press-a-button, solve-your-problem computer programs, one of the great contributions that psychology can bring is to help people *complicate* their understanding of human nature.

NOT KNOWING HOW TO SAY NO

Bill had consulted with Ed, the president of Marleine Securities for about eight years. Their relationship was a warm and close one, and Bill had helped Ed deal with many issues over the years, both of a personal and an organizational nature. One of Ed's frustrations that never seemed to get resolved, however, had to do with Woody Watson, the chief investment analyst. Woody was a brilliant man with a strong reputation in the industry who often acted like a prima donna in little ways that irritated Ed. Ed often spoke of his helpless anger and frustration at dealing with Woody, as well as his own embarrassment that he, the chief executive, could not seem to control this prima donna. He felt he was in an untenable position since Woody was so valuable to him and, yet, such a thorn in his side.

Bill had suggested numerous ways for Ed to constructively deal with Woody's apparent narcissism: pointing out how it affected Woody's image and effectiveness with others in the organization; pointing out how it embarrassed Ed, putting it in performance reviews; finding ways to meet Woody's needs more constructively so as to build reciprocity; etc. Woody generally acknowledged the reasonableness of what Ed said, but he usually had well-articulated rationalizations for each specific instance. Since each instance was usually different, it was difficult for Ed to make a clear case about Woody's underlying narcissism. In the course of Bill's consulting with Woody, he too tried to deal with the issue. Woody was basically receptive, at least on an intellectual level. He was usually sincere in his recognition that he was accountable for the problems his behavior caused. Yet, it was one area where Woody seldom showed signs of change.

One day, as Bill entered Ed's office, Ed was beaming, with just a touch of the look of the "cat that swallowed the canary." Ed said, "You know, Bill, in all the years you've worked with me, you have helped me a lot in a lot of areas, but I think you've had a blindspot—to use your word—about helping me deal with Woody. All the time, you've been trying to get me to be constructive about my anger toward Woody, and I think you've missed the point. Let me tell you what happened. Six weeks ago Woody parked in the visitors' parking area that is closest to the lobby, despite my clear policy that we must be gracious enough to leave the spaces open to our visitors. I did two things. First, I had Woody's car towed away. Second, I walked into Woody's office, I stared into his eyes, and I said, 'Don't you dare ever do anything like that again!' Then I walked right out, without letting him say a word. A week later, Woody came to me and told me that he was really sorry, and it was the first time I ever believed him. It has been six weeks, and he has been behaving himself like an altar boy. I should have done that years ago."

That evening, Bill was having dinner with his family. His five-year-old son, Mike, had, for the thousandth time, picked up his food with his fingers. Bill got up immediately, took Mike's plate, dumped it in the garbage disposal, and sent Mike to bed without supper.

Bill's father was a gentle, sensitive, overcontrolled, and quiet man who had been dominated by Bill's somewhat hysterical mother. Through his life, Bill had worked through many of his feelings of emasculation and, in many ways, had become an assertive person. But it had taken Ed to teach him how to put his foot down. All of Bill's advice had been for Ed to be objective and dispassionate, to "maturely" suppress his seething anger, rather than to be real. Bill's own tendencies toward appeasement and his fears of uncontrolled emotionality had prevented him from fully tuning into and respecting the constructiveness of Ed's anger. Had he done so, he could have helped Ed earlier to find an authentic means of getting through to Woody.

INTERNAL VIGILANCE

The particular "hookers" that diminish objectivity vary greatly from consultant to consultant. Here are some others:

- *Fear of hurting others,* leading to protecting people from the full truth. Such protection is often a form of disrespect because it signals that the receiver is too fragile, defensive, or immature to deal with straightforward feedback.

- *Fear of being explicit,* leading to a distaste of the concrete and a tendency to err in the direction of ambiguity and obfuscation.

- *Fear of controlling people's lives too much,* leading to hedging. The issue of manipulating "too much," of sharing and of *not* sharing accountability at the same time, is not a simple issue, but it is important for the consultant to decide just where his or her influence begins and ends, to sort out the ambiguity rather than to remain ambivalent.

- *Fear of confronting,* leading the consultant to let the client control too much of the relationship. The consultant needs to manage the consulting day and to scrupulously maintain the boundaries of the consulting relationship.

- *Rescuing,* which deprives people of the empowerment that solving their own problems affords. It is very tempting for the consultant to do because the consultant often has the power of access to upper management. Often, rescues imply villains and, by rescuing one individual, the consultant risks making another into a villain.

- *Authority problems,* leading to romanticized visions of organizational democracy, overidentification with underdogs, being too impressed by the powerful, overingratiation, or overreaction to legitimate control.

- *Impatience,* leading to pressing for action before people or organizations are ready, imposition of "progressive" values, or ineffective programmatic interventions.

- *Imposition of personal values,* such as rationalism, expansionism, or iconoclasm.

- *Fear of jeopardizing the relationship,* leading to inappropriate compromise and accommodation regarding standards, and giving the client what is asked for rather than what is needed.

- *Fear of being wrong,* leading to overly conservative recommendations about evaluated candidates, and to overgeneral or overqualified predictions.

There are many other possible sources of bias reflecting the values, behavioral predispositions, and unconscious motivations and defenses of each individual consultant (see Ross, 1977). The complexity of organizational life and the power of its rewards and punishments constantly test one's capacity to resist bias. Yet, often, the most enduring consulting contributions reflect the consultant's position as an outsider who brings objectivity and insight to the present to help people uncloud what lies on the horizon.

There are no easy answers about how to stay objective. Unfortunately, most of our foibles become most evident only after we have worked them through. All of us will err in objectivity much more than we would wish. And, programmed perfection can detract from being real. The discipline of inner scrutiny and the search for external feedback both help. Perhaps the greatest mistake we can make is forgetting the need to presume bias, and thus neglecting the need to keep a lamp shining within.

Belonging to a partnership of consulting psychologists helps. First, one's colleagues can provide personal feedback. Second, they can serve as sounding boards who share not only consulting experience, but often the historical context of a particular client relationship. Third, it is easier to be courageous and congruent with one's professional values when one is assured the consensual validation as well as the shared financial risk available from one's partners. Other options include professional development experiences, collegial roundtables, reading, and the like. Last, the discipline of listening carefully to the feedback one receives from one's clients is something from which we can all profit.

8

Juggling Multiple Roles

It is only shallow people who do not judge by appearances.
The true mystery of the world is the visible, not the invisible.
                            Oscar Wilde (*The Portrait of Dorian Gray*)

Psychotherapists try to maintain intimate awareness of the roles that they play in the therapeutic relationship and how their roles are perceived by clients. The realities of transference and countertransference lead us to attempt to sculpt the dimensions and boundaries of the therapist's role into a therapeutic relationship. In many little ways the therapist tries to separate the therapist-as-person from the therapist-as-therapist and to maintain a role that is, if not completely neutral, at least free of overriding personal agenda. The psychotherapist wonders, "Should I temper the heartiness of my laugh at that off-color joke? Is this gift too large to be a token? Is this hug of appreciation just a hug; should I allow it, and how expressively should I return it, if at all? Is this personal anecdote going to put too much focus on me?"

All therapists fall somewhere between role-sterilized neutrality and uninhibited personal authenticity, and most of us realize that there are costs and benefits in being at any particular place on the continuum. What is probably more important than where a particular therapist falls on the continuum is the degree to which the therapist consistently maintains an awareness of the continuum. Thus, excepting the schoolish ideologues, those who tend toward neutrality realize that they risk distancing, objectification, and intellectualization, whereas those who tend toward authenticity realize they risk role contamination, erosion of boundaries, and the seepage of the therapist's own psychic muck into the sanctum of the therapeutic relationship.

85

The proscribed nature of the psychotherapeutic relationship limits these risks to some extent. The scheduled, time-limited visit, the soundproofed walls and white noise, the prearranged comfortable seating, the social routines of the therapy hour, the way the session starts and ends, and the content of the discussion—all of these serve to confine the relationship and to bind the therapist and the client to their roles. In consulting, on the other hand, these bounds are necessarily more fluid; their containment lies less in situations and expectations than in the vigilance and scrupulousness of the consultant. Psychological consulting to management takes place "on the fly," in the client's environment, where what control the consultant achieves over the therapeutic situation is a result of consistent, conscious, active work rather than the habitual enactment of a prearranged and traditional ordering.

Controlling the client relationship takes work and sometimes requires ruffling of feathers. It means ensuring a confidential meeting place on the client company's premises, even if the client is philosophically committed to "open office" concepts. It means not allowing one's schedule to be automatically determined by someone in the personnel department who may be trying to help or who likes to feel in control, but it does mean retaining the flexibility to switch gears and to question the rationales for how one is being used. It means actively seeing to it that any company copies of the consultant's paperwork are maintained with utmost confidentiality. It means persuading the organization to allow the consultant a good deal of leeway in prioritizing how to spend consulting time, since the consultant, with an ear to the ground, is likely to know which areas are going to become hot before they do. The more resourcefully and the less reflexively consultants operate, the more they are able to leverage their unique perspective in identifying and reacting to issues that arise.

ENLIGHTENED SELF-INTEREST

In the business world, the consultant is expected to act *like a consultant,* and this differs from the expectations people have of therapists. The consultant is expected to sell, and he or she is presumed to have, at least, a touch more enlightened self-interest than the presumedly more altruistic therapist. The client, therefore, often maintains a degree of buyer's vigilance that is greater than what the therapist encounters in the psychotherapy relationship. In order to effectively address this vigilance, the consultant must first be clear that his or her own motivations are congruent with what the client needs. Next, it is important that the consultant not be uncomfortable either with the client's vigilance or with the fact of the consultant's own self-interest. By legitimizing the realities of the transaction, the consultant can now help the client sort out the costs and benefits of the consultant's services.

Billing, too, can be a problem. The consultant's bill is expected to be itemized, like every other bill the client receives. However, when the consultant explains that the requirements of confidentiality and sensitivity to therapeutic relationships preclude some itemization, such "shrinkiness" is often as barely indulged as it is respected. The consultant must walk the fine line between accommodating the client's legitimate needs and maintaining the sanctity of confidential relationships with individuals. The consultant must help the client understand that the mere knowledge that an individual has received consulting may jeopardize confidentiality. The greater the specificity of the consultant's bill, the greater the chance is of compromising long-term trust.

As a business person, the ways the consultant seeks and follows through with referrals to other clients demands more active involvement than the characteristic hands-off psychotherapeutic relationship. The ideal consulting relationship is one in which satisfied clients would continually provide a stream of referrals to the consultant, and the consultant would then never need to provide stimulation for referrals. However, many clients, especially those who do not come from sales or marketing backgrounds, may not think much about the consultant's need to make a living. Unlike the private psychotherapist who can rely upon many professional referral sources as well as former clients, the consultant's source of referrals is primarily the small pool of chief executives and senior managers with whom he or she has worked. Therefore, the consultant may have little choice but to attempt to stimulate referrals. In doing so, there are obviously some real dangers of potential contamination of relationships. Some consultants simply don't ask. Some limit referral requests to only a very small group, e.g., only the chief executives with whom they work. Some conduct referral-related conversations only in outside-the-company-walls contexts. Ultimately, of course, the "solution" rests on the basic integrity and openness of the consultant. To pretend such conversations don't potentially have an impact on a relationship, however, is simply unrealistic.

WEARING DIFFERENT HATS

The consultant must wear many hats, unless he or she chooses to narrowly specialize and to have an impact less broad and integrative. Yet, there are certain natural incompatibilities among the roles of therapist, sounding board, expert, and evaluator; and, which hat is being worn must be clear at all times, both to the consultant and to the client. For example, when the consultant is acting as an expert, as in feeding back to a hiring manager on the characteristics of an applicant, the consultant must meld the client's need for feedback with the additional need to help the manager to feel empowered in the hiring process. Similarly, the consultant must balance the evaluative role in making a judgment about someone's promotability with the need to help that individual deal with the ramifications of the consultant's evaluative judgment. This can be done when the consultant is absolutely clear with himself or herself as well as with the individual regarding the consultant's mixed agenda, and when the consultant is clear in the belief that the evaluative judgment will ultimately be in the best interests of the individual, even if it may cause temporary distress.

A number of other roles harbor potential conflicts. As a seminar lecturer, for example, or as a dinner guest during an overnight consulting engagement, it is often inappropriate *not* to share more of one's nonprofessional self. Yet, to do so without constraint may, ultimately, disserve the client. To the extent that the client finds discrepancies between his or her own projections and expectations and the therapist's revealed political or religious beliefs, social habits, or world view, the client must then contend with them once the professional relationship is resumed. An innocent tennis game during an exercise break at a seminar can lead to a variety of feelings, depending upon who wins. The consultant is clearly a human being with needs, so it is impossible to recommend that the consultant maintain complete role sterility by never eating with people or playing tennis at seminars. Yet, it is the peculiar burden of the psychological consultant to never lose sight of the possibility that his or her own excursions into nonconsultant roles may impose an unfair burden on the individuals to whom he or she consults. The therapeutic role must take precedence. No matter how informal the social situation, the consultant must maintain continual awareness of his or her own boundaries and the client's need for those boundaries to be maintained. Furthermore, the power of transferrence often leads the client to want more informal, social, and personal kinds of contact. The consultant, therefore, needs to continually weigh and balance what is in the longer-term best interests of the client.

CLARIFYING ALLEGIANCES

Even when role consistency is maintained, there is the problem of multiple allegiances and actual or perceived conflicts of interest. The individual is aware that the consultant has allegiances to others in the organization, and the individual has feelings about those allegiances. The consultant is almost always "not just mine, but someone else's—and that someone else may not have good intent toward me." I believe that defining *the individual* as the client as well as the strict maintenance of confidentiality are key to helping people cope with the consultant's multiple allegiances. It is, therefore, essential that the consultant's commitment to these principles be consistently demonstrated in many little ways: the respect the consultant shows for the subordinates or associates of an individual as their names come up in discussion with that individual, the strictness and fullness with which confidentiality is maintained, and the degree to which the consultant maintains nonjudgmental receptivity to opinions or actions that may be contrary to the interests of his or her other constituents.

Often, the consultant's willingness to reflect a position seemingly at odds with organizational mythology lets a person see that the consultant can be free of incompatible allegiances. For example, during periods of employee economic layoffs, few companies adequately address the issue of the guilt people feel, because they are so busy defending the correctness of their actions. It is often incumbent upon the consultant to put the guilt into words, as he or she helps an individual manager sort out feelings of guilt and betrayal of loyal subordinates. In so doing, the consultant is saying that, at least in the protected environs of the consulting relationship, the defensive group-think that characterizes the manager's other company associations will not be necessary. Without taking a position as to whether or not the lay-offs were justified, the consultant can acknowledge the manager's suppressed outrage in a manner that affirms the individual and his or her feelings. It affirms, as well, that the consultant answers to a sense of congruence, and not to a higher organizational power of a defensive organizational myth.

In a similar vein, it is wise to refuse to play the role of mediator when there are disputes. The consultant should make it clear that he or she will facilitate communication, but that it is not the consultant's role to settle anything or even to suggest a compromise. The consultant cannot have complete allegiance to an individual and then provide social pressure to force that person to compromise. It is one thing to *suggest* that one's client compromise; it is quite another to become an agent of the individual's environment who promotes that compromise.

Perhaps the perception to be most avoided is that the consultant is so allied with upper management as to require similar delicate handling. Since the consultant starts the relationship as "the president's bad idea," and as the consultant explicitly serves at the president's pleasure, people have ample reason to question whether the consultant, will, in the final analysis, put more weight on that allegiance than on others. It is probably impossible to dispel this fear completely because it is realistic and it is often based upon past experiences with consultants, some of whom may have been psychologists. Furthermore, it would be naive for an individual to assume without strong evidence that the psychologist has the integrity and objectivity as well as the intellectual subtlety to discern and take appropriate action in all instances where incompatible allegiances potentially exist. Some psychologists, believing that it cannot be done, proscribe strict procedural confinement as a means of ensuring objectivity. For example, they may simply define the "organization" as their client (usually meaning chief executive), or they may refuse to assume both evaluative and developmental roles. But, to me, objectivity is a quality of a person, not of a person's technique; therefore, mandating objectivity procedurally will but limit depth and scope.

The consultant's allegiances are projected through subtle nuances in behavior. Whether or not the consultant eats in the executive dining room, with whom the consultant sits and is seen, what privileges the consultant is allowed and whether these are privileges afforded to all visitors or to upper managers, whose organizational buzz words the consultant chooses to adopt (and, therefore, in whose tongue the consultant speaks), whose parking space or office the consultant borrows, what "insider information" the consultant proudly reveals—all affect the way the consultant will be perceived. There are real consequences to being seen as the president's Rasputin.

OTHER PROBLEMATIC ROLES

Another characterization to be avoided is that of Merlin the Magician. All psychotherapists are, at times, seen by clients as omniscient, but psychological consultants to management reinforce the perception by dazzling people with consistently correct predictions that seem to the untrained eye to emanate from the mystical sources of the consultant's inner genius. Given the adulation fortune tellers and astrologers receive, it is not surprising that psychological wizardry should achieve even greater acclaim. Unfortunately, just as people succumb to illusions of control over uncertainty with the "quacks," so can they do with consultants. An occasional moment of private exultation about one's "guruness" is best allowed to fade out and the client brought back into focus. Not only will the image of omniscience create dependency and prevent empowerment, but the consultant may well later become entrapped in a web of oracular expectations. At times, and in some ways, clients may need us to be a little perfect; I am merely suggesting that we not be larger-than-life.

The potential role of ombudsman is another difficult role to avoid. Often, people expect that the psychologist will carry the right messages about problems in the organization to the appropriate members of senior management. There is a triple danger here. First, to the extent that the consultant is perceived as a conduit of information—albeit a benevolent one—the perception of strict confidentiality erodes. Second, to the extent that the consultant solves people's problems for them, they do not grow. Third, as an ombudsman, the consultant becomes more an active player on the organizational stage and less a neutral, objective outsider to whom one can retreat from the main action.

Another image problem occurs when the psychologist is seen as a *fixer* to whom managers send their "problem kids." Sometimes helping the "problem" individual is well-targeted and is not a matter of doing for the manager what the manager should be doing for the individual. Nevertheless, the consultant can become so identified with "problem kids" that people fail to see how their own issues might apply, or they stay away from the consultant to avoid the stigma. Similarly, consultants will be perceived as *angels of death* if they are always conspicuous just before someone is fired. The consultant may well have much to offer to the individual and to management—it is the conspicuousness that may need to be tempered.

Since practitioners in the psychological professions often tend to be expressive and tolerant of nonpathological social deviance, there is the possibility that a certain looseness can lead the consultant to be seen as a "flake," "odd-ball," or "nutcake." Some people expect "shrinks" to be this way, whereas others enjoy exposing the Achilles' heels of those who arouse their fear or ambivalence. Both types of people can turn minute indiscretions or mannerisms into counterproductive company legends. The too-old-fashioned, too-casual, or too-flamboyant manner of dress; the unkempt beard; the routinized dietary ritual; the cognitive looseness inherent in puns; the overuse of jargon; the hardly-noticeable twitch; the touch of arrogance; the revelation of one's sexual permissiveness with one's children; and the too-often-told anecdote—all have a way of becoming overblown and, in turn, reframing the image of the consultant. There are, of course, times when the consultant can use his or her own deviations to make a point and, perhaps, there are reasonable limits to the willingness to suppress individuality; yet, ultimately, the consultant will be accountable for the ripples in the consulting relationship that his or her individuality creates.

THE CONSULTING PSYCHOLOGIST AS MENTAL HEALTH CRISIS WORKER

One advantage of maintaining an image of a psychologist who is "shrinky but not *so* shrinky" is that people who might otherwise be reluctant to seek mental health services may be willing to talk to the consultant. The fact that the consultant is on the site also helps. Often, the referral to the consultant can be made by the person's supervisor or through the personnel department, if it is aware of the problem. Naturally, a number of people will view the consultant as too enmeshed with their employer, and will seek help elsewhere. However, I have found that the consultant can be helpful to quite a few people who, otherwise, would not seek help at all. Typically, I act as a referral source by helping the individual see that he or she has a problem that can be dealt with and suggesting a person to see. Sometimes simply helping to assess the problem, reframing it, or prescribing some stress management approaches is all that is needed to prevent a stress management problem from being diagnosed and treated as a medical one, for example.

Often there is an opportunity to use the consultant's unique vantage point to work with a person's supervisor as well as with the individual, and this is an opportunity grossly ignored by most practicing psychotherapists. Lower level workers, in particular, are very frequently apt to underestimate the capacity of their supervisors to behave humanely and generously in times of personal crisis. Their fear is exacerbated when they have already been criticized for poor performance. Therapists unfamiliar with the workplace, especially when they carry emotional baggage and preconceptions regarding callousness or authoritarianism in business, often misdiagnose career problems based on the misperceptions their clients relate to them. There is, then, a great opportunity for the consultant to bring skill and objectivity to bear and to work with the system in helping people overcome their difficulties. Similarly, the consultant can be a useful resource to provide background and make appropriate connections for an individual's private therapist. This is assuming that the individual thinks to tell the therapist of the resource or that the therapist happens to ask whether the individual's company employs a psychological consultant. Additionally, the consultant is able to use the vantage point of a particular person's crisis to help the organization explore whether or not more fundamental issues need to be addressed, such as the quality of employee selection and placement practices, the adequacy of supervisory training, and the utility of company support and referral systems.

9

Are Management Psychology Seminars Worthwhile?

Into each life some confusion should come . . . also some enlightenment.
And my voice goes everywhere with you, and changes into the voice of your parents, your teachers, your playmates and the voices of the wind and of the rain. . . .
Milton H. Erickson (*A Teaching Seminar with Milton H. Erickson*[1])

The answer to the question posed by the title of this chapter is, of course, "yes and no." There is a legitimate, healthy skepticism about seminars, because many people come away from them enthused or even elated, without having fundamentally changed psychodynamically or behaviorally. Some of the sensitivity groups like those of the 1960s, for example, have become much less prevalent—not so much because of their "casualty" rates, but because of the evanescence of their effects. However, some seminars can be potentially valuable.

Management seminars by psychologists tend to focus on one or more of a fairly wide range of topics including self-development, employee development, effective leadership, decision making, team building, communication, interviewing, and stress management. They typically consist of some combination of lecture and discussion with participant-involving exercises. They can be massed or spaced, short or long, home or away, in-house or "stranger," homogeneous or heterogeneous. Some seminars tend to focus more on "education" whereas others focus more on "growth." I have never really figured out the difference between the two, unless it is that education is what it was when people have not changed!

A major problem with many seminars is similar to one shared by the increasingly abandoned traditional state mental hospitals founded in the nineteenth century. Just as the mental patients were unable to learn community coping skills sheltered away from the community, it is similarly improbable that individuals will carry back much of value from a seminar taken in isolation. Rather, those seminars that are a part of an integrated whole are most likely to lead to lasting change. Success is greatest when the seminar's purpose is consistent with explicit company goals, when a critical mass of seminar graduates return "home," when the organizational culture encourages learning and growing, when there is follow-up that constantly reinforces the mentality and performance the seminar attempts to create. Management must explicitly, tangibly, visibly, and consistently promote, support, and reward the kinds of changes the seminar attempts to achieve. One way that senior managers can demonstrate their own commitment is to participate in the seminars. It is also important that people know why they are there and, especially, that the seminar be presented in constructive terms rather than as a means for correcting liabilities.

Some seminars feature preconceived notions, authoritatively based on questionable research about, for example, what it takes to be a good manager, a good leader, or a good communicator. Participants take tests presumedly measuring concordance with the ideal. Unfortunately, I have had to spend many hours debriefing horrified managers whose successful styles happened not to accord with someone's pet template.

Seminars are at their most dangerous when they provide false comfort, either because they mask real problems by defining causes superficially, or because they divert people from more fundamental solutions. If the process of a seminar is faddish or superficial, then the culture may be deluded into assuming that it is prepared for change. Seminars can also be harmful when they are based on shallow models of human behavior. For example, transactional analysis, despite its distinct virtues in explaining the accountabilities in communication, is sometimes presented as if it is an encompassing model of human behavior, which it is not. Amidst a torrent of psycho-babble, participants are encouraged to see human behavior superficially and to apply techniques of pseudo-authenticity to co-workers rather than simply to understand them and to let understanding itself give birth to action. Easy taxonomies and simplistic psychologies are popular because they give people quick relief from ambiguity. The irony is that perhaps the most important contribution psychology can make is to lead people away from such golden calves and toward the ambiguity, which is, after all, where the action is. *In context,* simplification can help people orient toward the complex and the ambiguous; *out of context,* it hides them. Models of man, like stars, are beacons to the beyond; when, in a mortal instant, we turn them into gods, they cease to illuminate (see Dagenais, 1972; Hampden-Turner, 1981).

WHAT GOOD CAN
PSYCHOLOGICAL SEMINARS DO?

One of the most common achievements of just about any good psychologically oriented seminar is the reinforcement of the concept of psychological causality. One reason we professionals have come to our field is that we tend to see psychological causality more vividly than the average person. For us, it stands out from the background in contrasting colors, whereas other people tend to operate as if color blind. Yet, most people can learn to be more comfortable using their capacities for psychological-mindedness. Most important, they can become increasingly compelled by the ideas that *psychological causation is a human constant* and that *they are accountable for its effects.* Most human solutions in organizations boil down to these two ideas; the rest is mainly a matter of technique. It is virtually fruitless to try to teach managers to develop their people, to interview applicants, or to effectively manage their interpersonal relationships until the ideas of psychological causality and accountability have ripened in their minds. These concepts must, therefore, constitute the core of any psychological seminar, no matter what the apparent subject matter. Only as these core concepts mature will people be empowered to use the rest.

Large ideas take time to work their way in. Seminars need to be long enough so that participants can walk away with new ideas and not just lists of psychological trivia that are soon junked. For example, a seminar on interviewing needs to make the point that participants can get the most useful data from open-ended questions. It often takes two or three days to make that point stick. Instead of focusing on what to *do,* the focus needs to be on making sense of the data. Once people begin to appreciate what they need to know, they then begin to realize what questions they must ask to get there. These concepts are seldom what participants expect, but by giving them what they expect, how can they be expected to *change their minds?* As William James said, "An idea, to be suggestive, must come to the individual with the force of a revelation."

Regardless of their surface content, psychological seminars are opportunities for self-examination and personal growth. As anyone who has taught abnormal psychology has found, the continuities of human behavior are such that when almost anything psychological is discussed, people will compare and contrast with themselves. Therefore, I try to design opportunities for self-examination into the fabric of seminars. The vehicle of seminars can sometimes lead to less resistance to insight, since the focus is usually on someone else. Seminars offer opportunities to jumble up preconceptions through new ideas or revealing exercises. They are often similar to religious retreats in that they take people away from the daily clamor and clip, and they offer a chance for reflection, even solitude. For these reasons, there are distinct advantages to seminars that are somewhere away from the workplace, where there are no interruptions, where people stay overnight, where there are small comforts or woods to walk in. Thus conceived, the consultant can use the medium of the seminar consciously with psychotherapeutic intent. In the tradition of Milton Erickson (Zeig, 1980), a seminar can be conducted on more than one level. Seminars provide rich opportunities for psychotherapeutic metamessages and metaexperiences that are, in any case, best received obliquely.

When seminars are repeatedly given to many people within an organization, a common language usually evolves for discussing the "soft" phenomena about which people are usually incredibly inarticulate. Eventually, the process of seminars and the evolution of new meanings can add new dimensions to the organization's consciousness. As more and more individuals become more psychologically minded, this mentality becomes the cultural norm. As a result, performance reviews begin to be done with greater depth; growth is seen as a psychological process and not just one of technical education or the meeting of objectives; and the organization begins to look more at means rather than just focusing on ends.

---

1. From *A teaching seminar with Milton H. Erikson* (p. vii), by J. K. Zeig, copyright © 1980 by The Milton H. Erikson Foundation. Reprinted by permission of the publisher.

10

Internal or External Consulting?

In giving advice seek to help, not to please, your friend.
Solon (seventh–sixth century B.C.)

Although most psychological consultants have historically worked as independent practitioners, some consultants now operate as internal consultants for a single organization. Just as many organizations have tried to cut costs by hiring internal attorneys and other professionals, some see the advantage in hiring internal psychological consultants. Furthermore, as the professionalism and credibility of human resources departments have improved, often at the urging of management psychologists, companies have been increasingly willing to spend dollars to expand the services provided by such departments.

Cost containment is probably the greatest advantage of using internal consultants. The second advantage is that the internal consultant may be given the power to implement certain programs or procedures, whereas the external consultant must rely on persuasion alone. Third, an expanding inhouse consulting capacity may help foster continuity as well as deeper organizational exposure to psychological-mindedness. Psychology becomes part of an organization's selfidentity in a way that may be more tangible than simply relying on an external resource.

Although there are significant contributions that can be made by internal consultants, the kind of consulting described in this book is, very simply, more easily done by outside consultants. It is beyond the scope of this book to discuss the many areas where internal consulting is the sounder solution. In particular, when they are aware of the kinds of pitfalls they may encounter, they can design their interventions to avoid them (see Hall, 1976; Kahn et al., 1964; Klegon, 1978; Raelin, 1986).

THE OUTSIDER'S LEVERAGE

Whether or not it is merited, the outside consultant tends to be perceived as more objective, more competent, broader in scope, and less personally involved than the internal consultant. Outside professionals are presumed to bring added value to the job by virtue of the diversity of their on-going experience. They have reputations beyond the organization, and their employment by others validates their worth. Internal consultants, on the other hand, are often perceived as not being able to "make it" in the real world. Their reputations may be unfavorably distorted by associations with other human resources executives in the organization. Their habits, idiosyncracies, and foibles are likely to be very well known within the organization, whereas most of the "dirty laundry" of the external consultant is confined to the outside consulting firm.

The exercise of power by an external consultant is necessarily always indirect. The outsider has less inherent power to abuse than the insider. The insider is likely to be held accountable for concrete or short-term actions or changes and is likely to have a turf to protect. This can lead to competitiveness, pulling rank, or other actions that will at least be perceived as self-serving, self-justifying, or empire-building. The outsider, on the other hand, is a head without a body, ideas without action. As a result, the outsider has little choice but to allow others accountability for their actions, freedom to make mistakes, and room to grow in their own ways. The outsider gains influence only as his or her constituency feels empowered.

THE OUTSIDER'S PERSPECTIVE

Objectivity cannot be assured simply by procedurally legislating it; nevertheless, some conditions are more likely to sustain an objective perspective and others are more likely to distort it. Being an outsider will tend to sustain it. First and foremost, the outsider is literally "outside" and can see the organization from a distance. To be objective, insiders must project themselves to the outside, and with this mental extrapolation there is always the chance of error. Insiders are most likely to be biased in perceiving those parts of the system that are at closest range. The internal consultant grows accustomed to, and therefore, may cease to notice, bumps and hollows that define the organizational terrain, and may take for granted certain organizational myths. When the organization is in turmoil, the internal consultant is less able to contextualize the turmoil, and is thereby subject to overreacting to it. When the organization experiences pain or fear or uncertainty, the insider experiences a part of that pain, fear, or uncertainty. He or she does not have the luxury of James Joyce's artist (*Portrait of the Artist as a Young Man*), who "remains . . . invisible, refined out of existence, indifferent, paring his fingernails."

The external consultant is able to see the issues of a client organization in comparison with those of their own organizations. There is little problem of calibration since the consultant's breadth of experience provides bench marks within which to contextualize issues and events. The longer the tenure of an insider, the more the insider will see events through filters based on one organization's experiences. In contrast, the external consultant can juxtapose observations among a larger array of clients as well as with colleagues within one's own firm. Particularly for external consultants who are part of a group, colleagues who are out of the client company system and who have no ax to grind can often provide the very perspective that is least apparent and most important. The objective perspectives of one's colleagues also allows collegial support and consensual validation to mean more to the consultant than the inputs of those with greater emotional involvement. One's colleagues also provide an atmosphere that helps the consultant frame a professional identity outside of one's clients and, it is hoped, one's colleagues provide the nurturance, feedback, and stimulation that foster professional development.

THE PREROGATIVES OF POWER

The internal consultant is subordinate, at least to the chief executive officer, and often to others within the organization. As a result, the consultant is diminished in the eyes of superiors, and doubts about the consultant's objectivity are raised in the minds of all others who are apt to assume that the consultant does the bidding of his or her superiors. The superiors are less able to fully let their hair down and be truly vulnerable, and they are more likely to see the insider's input as "just" another organizational opinion. Others in the organization will have difficulty trusting that the inside consultant's objectivity is not influenced by competing agenda, and they will certainly have difficulty fully believing that *they* are the insider's client and that their relationship would supercede an allegiance to the insider's boss or organization. As a result, the insider may receive highly filtered input designed to mask vulnerability or error, to impress the consultant, to strategically plant information, or to put a particular spin on the interpretation of an event.

The outside consultant is not only *perceived* as having fewer organizational axes to grind, but in reality this is the case. There is a vast difference between being a servant and being a subordinate. The servant who is also a subordinate is precisely positioned to better please the superior. In consulting, where *serving* sometimes means *not pleasing* the client, the pressure to please puts stress on the consultant's ability to see and to act on what is most professionally sound. Senior managers can be rather intimidating even to outsiders; the possibility of intimidation greatly increases within the boss-subordinate relationship. Worse yet, the potential for disillusionment to contaminate the relationship is far greater when one is exposed to the seamier side of one's client and one's client is also one's boss.

Even if we were to assume that the consultant could fully separate serving and pleasing, the consultant's superior(s) will bring into the relationship certain expectations (see Berger, Cohen, & Zelditch, 1966) regarding the behavior of subordinates, and these expectations—mostly not conscious—are likely to lack the salutary respectful distance afforded to outsiders. When the outsider stands his or her ground for professional reasons, this "stubbornness" is likely to be perceived with respect, albeit grudging; the same behavior by an insider is likely to be perceived as insubordination. Since senior managers tend not to easily receive "back talk," the already difficult job of confronting one is rendered much more complicated when he or she is your superior. It is impossible for either the superior or the subordinate consultant to fully emerge from the tangles of their power relationship. These relationships are expressed in a multitude of ways—who sits where; who interrupts whom; who speaks loudest; who touches whom; who has what rights for initiating and ending conversations; who feels beholden to whom—and it is hard to imagine two individuals consistently able to transcend these expectations, even in the United States, where there is more apparent ambiguity, informality, and flexibility in such roles than in most other societies.

THE INSIDER'S BURDEN

The internal consultant is part of the action, dependent on company fortunes for a livelihood, and often tied into profit sharing or stock option programs that link company performance to personal security and wealth. The internal consultant has the pressure of having to live with the consequences of the actions of his or her own clients. As a result, each mistake that is made, each personality conflict that occurs, each time a person is psychologically stuck, may potentially reduce the inside consultant's own sense of personal safety and level of gratification and partially color the inside consultant's judgment. As Aesop said (in "The Fox and the Goat"), "Never trust the advice of a man in difficulties." In contrast, to the extent that the outside consultant is less ego-identified with a particular client and less dependent upon the client for personal and financial security and fulfillment, he or she is less apt to be personally invested in and biased by what goes on.

All of the insider's eggs are in one organizational basket. When times are tough, most of the consultant's clients are experiencing tough times. This can be a heavy burden on the insider who now needs to deal with everyone experiencing frustration similar to his or her own. On the other hand, the outside consultant is likely to be confronted at any one time with clients who are experiencing widely divergent fortunes, and when times are tough for the consultant there is little likelihood that a client will be simultaneously experiencing similar difficulty. In this way, the external consultant will tend to experience a balance of ups and downs of career and is less apt to catastrophize when what the client needs is balance. Even external consultants are subject to such difficulties when their clients predominate in a particular industry or geographical region that is undergoing hard times—or when the scope of their consulting is limited to a very few clients.

Much of consulting involves telling people what they do not want to hear—and often at the very moment they most want not to hear it. Sometimes the right thing to do is to terminate an account or to do that which will result in the termination of the account. Yet, for the insider, this may well mean losing one's job and one's livelihood. What is often required is simple courage. Yet, the decision to be courageous is not nearly as simple as the act. It must be made amidst murky uncertainties and countervailing forces. There are often good reasons to be pragmatic, to accept the client's agenda without superimposing the consultant's ideals. It is hard enough to try to figure out when to take a stand and when to go with the flow without being burdened with intense personal concerns. The larger such personal concerns loom, the greater are the chances of both rationalized appeasement and adolescent rebellion.

11

Managing a Consulting Psychology Practice

Good counselors lack no clients.
Shakespeare (*Measure for Measure*)

SETTING THE FEE

Psychological consultants, as well as most other consultants, tend to charge clients on a per diem basis. Some charge differentially based upon the kind of service provided. Some charge different clients differentially. Some charge differentially among professionals within the firm, depending upon experience, expertise, seniority, or other factors. Some charge for incidental time, such as account management and coordination, travelling time, incidental phone calls, and the like; others add an override to their fee to cover such charges; some do not charge for incidentals at all. On an hourly basis, management psychologists charge anywhere from less than the "going" rate for psychotherapy to two or even three times that rate, per actual service hour. Expenses are typically billed as accrued or with a percentage override added. There are no firm guidelines or precedents to follow.

Too high a fee can result in the perception that the service is overpriced or that the consultant is exploitive. Perhaps most likely, it can lead the client to purchase only those services that are most easily understood or which have the clearest short-term payback. A client may be willing, for example, to pay a high price for psychological evaluations for candidates for executive positions, but balk at paying the same fees for ongoing consulting of a developmental nature. Too low a fee suggests lack of self-confidence or lack of genuine value on the part of the practitioner.

It is important to clarify fee policies to clients up front in order to avoid later misunderstanding, especially since clients are sometimes wary of the possibility of gouging by outside professionals. Rapid inflation and concomitant fee increases or tough times for the client company can tend to stimulate such concerns.

A major reason that pricing may surface as an issue is personal discomfort or an apologetic attitude on the part of the consultant. In arriving at pricing decisions, the consultant will need to sort out and distinguish between issues of client perception and market reaction versus the consultant's own standards of morality and of value. In other words, the psychological consultant's thoughts about what the fee should be might include: the "market" rate, the "value" of his or her time and experience and expertise, the client's perception of value, tempered by an estimate of the client's *and* the psychologist's sense of what is reasonable and fair. At the one extreme, the psychologist does not want to be lumped into the same perceptual pie with other high-priced specialists whose costs are seen as exorbitant and require monitoring and limiting. At the other extreme, overly low rates may, in fact, cause the client to undervalue the consultant. As with psychotherapy, or any other service for that matter, client complaints about fees are often signals that something else is amiss in the relationship.

BILLING THE CLIENT

For a variety of reasons, it is usually inappropriate for the psychologist's bill to specify in detail how consulting time is spent in an organization. The odds are that a number of people in any organization will see the bill, even if it is just sent to one person, and the groundrules of confidentiality mandate that the question of who spent time with the psychologist be a private matter. Similarly, it is inappropriate to potentially place an individual in the position of having to account for every minute spent with the psychologist. In addition, there is simply the issue of trust—given the profound and sensitive nature of the consulting relationship, something is amiss if the organization cannot assume the psychologist is putting time to appropriate use. Finally, there are two practical considerations. First, the typical consulting day involves so many contacts of such varied duration with so many people that it is impractical to specify every contact. The nature of the consultation is obviously misunderstood if such itemization is requested. Second, any attempt at specificity usually arouses more questions than it resolves.

Ideally, just one figure is provided, and it is billed to an account within the office of the chief executive officer. However, with the growing emphasis on decentralization in many companies, a number of companies find lump summing to be inconsistent with their culture and therefore unacceptable. As a result, it is sometimes necessary to allocate bills among profit or cost centers. In agreeing to do so, it needs to be made clear that the chief executive officer's account will be used to imbed any charges that might otherwise lead to the possibility of compromising confidentiality. Certain specific activities, such as seminars or evaluations of candidates, can be billed separately without endangering confidentiality; however, they have the disadvantage of initiating a process that down the road can lead to itemization. Too much itemization also has the drawback of making specific events appear as if they can be separated from the larger relationship. The consultant should avoid reinforcing such piecemeal thinking, whether in respect to the consulting relationship or to any other situation that fragments the client's perspective.

Most firms send the bills directly to the chief executive officer of the company. In this way, they reinforce the idea that the consulting relationship is a company-wide priority and that the consultant's allegiance is not to any particular department, such as the human resources department. Implicitly, it is also a reminder that "the sunflowers turn toward the sun," "that fish stink from the top down," that the character of an organization and its ability to evolve is in great part a reflection of the personalities of the chief executive officer and his or her immediate staff.

SELLING CONSULTING SERVICES

Ideally, selling consulting services is the same as selling psychotherapy. The initial session is an opportunity for the therapist to listen, to understand, and to provide hope to the client that something helpful can be achieved. In a sense, that is all there is to it.

There are a number of factors that make selling consulting not quite so simple. First, the selling is probably done on the client's premises. Second, the potential client may look at the consultant less like a helper and more like a vendor. Third, helping professionals have all sorts of feelings about *selling* being exploitive, selfish, unhumanitarian, or beneath a professional's dignity. Fourth, despite the reality that psychotherapy is an art of persuasion, many psychotherapists lack confidence in their ability to sell. Fifth, for appropriate and genuine reasons of ethics, psychotherapists tend to characteristically err in the direction of self-restraint lest their powers of persuasion generate false hopes. Sometimes, this can lead to a non-involving, inarticulate passivity that serves neither client nor therapist. All of these factors can lead the consultant to fail to do what would otherwise come naturally, namely to respond helpfully to the client's concerns. In any case, most initial sales are really solidified only later, after the consultant has had a chance to be helpful and to bring added value to the organization.

MARKETING PSYCHOLOGICAL CONSULTING SERVICES

There are many factors that contribute to the marketplace's reluctance to seek out psychological consulting. Much of the marketplace is uneducated. Many are unaware of the kinds of services psychological consultants provide and may not see the connection between their particular problems and psychological solutions. For those with some passing familiarity, the connection may be so vague that the potential consumer sees psychological consulting as a longshot. The effects of consulting are often seen as intangible by consumers who tend to emphasize clear objectives and the bottom line. Psychological consulting *is* less tangible in its process and its measureability. Our appropriate refusal to promise too much contrasts with the quick fixes offered by countless illusion peddlers to consumers who are sometimes dizzied by the rush to quarterly profits. We suffer from being seen as flaky, "shrinky," impractical, unrealistic, ivory tower, expensive, and insensitive to cost. We are associated with abnormality and deviance and are kept at bay by those who feel "just fine, thank you." Those who need us the most are often too rigid to seek us out, or they define problems in the nonpsychological terms they understand and seek solutions that are consonant, if not growthful. We most often seek to gain the ear of chief executives because change and growth require support from the top down to stick. Yet, chief executives are one of the most sales resistant and least accessible populations of consumers. They are often, by nature, independent, wary individuals who have learned to trust their own counsel.

What has worked best is relying upon satisfied clients to make referrals and then providing a quality of service that builds each account and generates more referrals. This is easiest to do if one joins an existing consulting firm with an established base of referral sources. Over the long haul, perceived helpfulness among clients should translate into referrals. Yet, it *feels* passive to rely upon a sales force of chief executives who may or may not have the inclination, the competence, or the occasion to make the needed referral. It has therefore been difficult for psychological consultants to grab hold of their futures in the way that other businesses and consultants do.

The Supreme Court decisions of the 1970s opened the way for professionals to advertise and led to a greater consciousness of marketing issues among helping professionals. A number of marketing consultants now specialize in the professional services, and a number of publications address the issue (see Connor & Davidson, 1985; Kotler & Bloom, 1984; Webb, 1982; Wheatley, 1983; Wilson, 1972; also see *Journal of Professional Services Marketing*). Their methods include market surveys, strategic positioning, brochure creation and enhancement, image building, advertising, networking, direct mailing and newsletters, giving speeches and seminars, and writing and being written about. Whether or not such approaches are worth the effort in psychological consulting to management has yet to be proved. What appears least understood is how to create an appreciation among potential consumers unfamiliar with management psychology for the many ways their needs could be effectively met.

TERMINATING OR REFUSING ACCOUNTS

Client relationships end when there is no longer a sufficient overlap of common purposes to justify continuing the relationship. There must be a good faith understanding between the consultant and the chief executive officer or other key contacts at a client organization. Lacking it, the consultant cannot know whether his or her interventions will ultimately help and not hurt people.

A number of years ago, a psychologist consulted to a small company after the president had called regarding difficulties he was having with one of his vice presidents. After working with these individuals a few times over a couple of months, the president decided to fire the vice president, and the consulting relationship "faded out." About once a year for the next few years something would come up—a conflict, an employee who was a candidate for a promotion, an issue of employee theft—and the consultant was able to be helpful in each isolated instance. However, he found himself having misgivings about whether he was truly serving the individuals in the organization. He felt there could easily come a time when, by allowing himself to respond to isolated events, he might become an unwitting participant in an abuse of power. He was responding this way in part because he knew the president to be highly critical of others, very apt to rationalize and to self-justify, and insensitive to his own accountabilities in his interpersonal transactions. The consultant was concerned that without a greater scope of relationship, and the possibility of helping the president to come to terms with his own accountabilities, he could somehow fall into the trap of becoming the president's hatchet-man. It had not happened, and the consultant did not know that it would happen. He did, however, use the occasion of one of the president's isolated calls to explain that he could only continue to serve in good conscience if they could establish a firmer and more formal basis for the consulting relationship. He has not heard from the president since. As happened in the case of the Neppo Corporation (Chapter 7), the company that wanted to use the psychologist as the vehicle for going back on its promise to employees, the consultant may have to refuse or terminate an account in order not to let the client organization make unsound use of the consultant's services.

Sometimes a client organization reaches a stage of status quo, where little happens that justifies continued consulting. Whatever the causes, or the potentially adverse future consequences, the consultant may well need to opt out, perhaps to be called upon again when circumstance next jiggles the client organization's system. If the consultant stays on too long, the consultant's natural bias toward growth, fulfillment, and maximization of potentials may destabilize a system that has on its own decided to set anchor in order to achieve equilibrium—a decision the consultant must respect. For example, a consultant had been dealing with an industry association about, among other issues, the serious restraints imposed upon the association by its member companies. These restraints prevented the association from expanding services which would have allowed the association to become independently profitable and less dependent upon member companies. The consultant worked with the association president on the best strategies for persuading the board to recognize the dilemma as well as on some of the personal inhibitions the president had. The effort eventually failed, dooming the association to a stagnant "maintenance mode." Though there were still issues to be dealt with, the consultant and the president eventually agreed that the consulting relationship should be drastically reduced, since growth and fundamental changes were impossible.

Whatever the circumstances that end the consulting relationship, if the relationship has been intense and of reasonable length, the consultant is likely to experience feelings of loss and depression. If the termination resulted from the consultant's failure or the organization's failure, the consultant needs to grapple with the issues of self-esteem that may arise. Even when the termination results from more capricious circumstances, such as a take-over and management change dictated more by Wall Street maneuvers than by company soundness, the consultant nevertheless will wonder if there were a way that he or she could have made a difference. Even with perfectly clean "scorecards," consultants who lose accounts lose an opportunity to be at their best, to express their talents with a receptive constituency. Consultants, being fairly independent types, may tend to minimize the psychological toll that such losses take on them, which may lead to nonconstructiveness on other fronts. Consultants are wise, then, to look inside themselves for the small signs—the too-strong sense of urgency that betrays a hint of underlying dread, the too-critical or too-perfectionistic stance that masks the fury, the too-grandiose posture or the self-serving display to fill the void, the ingratiating flinch of appeasement to gain acceptance (where steely confrontation was the order of the day)— that help identify the intrapsychic work they need to do.

DEALING WITH OTHER PSYCHOLOGICAL CONSULTANTS

Consultants encounter each other within the same organization for a variety of reasons. Different consultants, often from the same firm, may consult with different divisions or sub-units of the larger organization. Psychological evaluations of candidates may be scheduled with someone other than the consultant of record for reasons of timeliness, or geographical proximity. One consultant or firm of consultants may offer a seminar to another consultant's client.

Clearly, the guiding rule ought to be to serve the best interests of the client organization, whether the "other" consultant is in one's own firm or is an outsider. There is a need to achieve as much consistency as possible in confidentiality practices, psychological study procedure, format of the written study, calibration of recommendations of candidates, definition of client issues, consulting methods, and related areas. Unfortunately, different consultants may vary widely in these practices, often reflecting the different perspectives of their original disciplines and sub-disciplines. In some cases, they are potentially in direct competition with one another but it is hoped that they can achieve sufficient coordination so as to keep client interests foremost and to prevent confusion.

Even within a single firm, divergences need to be sorted out. Typically, it is best to have a single overall account coordinator who maintains active interest and involvement with all aspects of the client relationship. The sharing of various perspectives about the client can yield greater insight, especially into those issues about which there may be differences among subparts of the organization. One potentially highly charged synapse within organizations is that between the corporate entity and its divisions, and this separation is often mirrored in the different consulting activities among members of one firm serving the same account. Thus, the primary account coordinator often has greatest contact with the corporate perspective, whereas his or her colleagues may share the perspective of the divisions subordinate to the corporate entity. The issues of subordination that play themselves out within the organization may also play themselves out among the consultants and these issues are best addressed by the consultants lest they identify so closely with their client's perspectives as to reify rather than help resolve the nonconstructive energies at the point of synapse.

Clients are often very sensitive to the issue of being shunted off from a trusted consultant to one of the "juniors" in his or her firm. It is common practice among legal, accounting, and consulting firms to do so, and it is often done with little regard for clients' needs and sensitivities. The first solution to this problem is for a firm to select uniformly good people. A second remedy is to ensure that decisions to involve other consultants are made for reasons beyond the fact that the consulting firm wants to expand, and then to air these reasons with the client. Third, the new colleague will be less likely to be perceived as a "junior" if the primary consultant works hard to change—and not to consciously or unconsciously reinforce—that perception. This is not always easy for the primary consultant to do, since the situation and the primary consultant's unconscious needs may both work toward reinforcing the subordinate status of the new colleague.

There can be a great advantage for the client organization in a fresh perspective, in having a back-up consultant who is concerned and knowledgeable about the client, and in being able to offer individuals the freedom of choosing the particular consultant with whom they feel most comfortable. The primary consultant must manage the account to allay the client's fears about being exploited (for the benefit of the consulting firm); otherwise the client may be deprived of potentially worthwhile benefits of multiple consultants.

THE CULTURE OF THE CONSULTING FIRM

The consulting firm within which a consultant practices can play an important part in the individual consultant's personal sense of well-being as well as his or her ability to respond to client needs. The consulting firm is a source of client referrals and shared financial risk. It can be a place to let one's hair down, to share stories, to brag, and to come home to. It can be a place to cross-fertilize, to be stimulated, and to receive consensual validation for decisions or practices done in lonely isolation. In addition to their individual consulting experience, firm members can benefit from the collective experience that has accrued over the life span of the firm.

The firm can be a place in which to grow up, to learn the trade, to be mentored, and to receive the kind of feedback that only concerned colleagues can provide (see Rogers, 1969; Schein, 1973; Schon, 1987, pp. 82–93). It can be a place to meet the genuine needs a consultant has that cannot or should not be met within the context of the client relationship: the need to belong to and identify with an organization, the need to manage or mentor others, the need *not* to have to administer the details of one's practice, the need to sow one's seeds and pass on one's best skills, the need to directly achieve tangible goals or organizational growth for which one is personally accountable, the need to reach out to areas beyond one's specific profession, and the like. A consulting firm can provide an environment for constructively playing out those issues that arise within the course of one's life cycle and its transitions, from the time of apprenticeship through the winding down, and with all the trials—personal and professional—in between.

The firm can provide, in the end, for the continuance of one's work through the contributions made to colleagues, as well as through the firm's ability to carry on and sustain the momentum achieved in client organizations.

The firm may also allow its consultants an opportunity to express and work through their own "hot spots" involved with being an individual in an organization: issues of subordination and dominance; expansion and restriction; structure and spontaneity; joining and individuation; autonomy and cooperation; compromise, competition, and conflict; idealism, pragmatism, and realism. As consultants successfully grapple with these issues, their perspectives on organizational life are widened. And, as they themselves grow as people, their perceptions become more accurate.

On the other hand, a firm managed with priorities superordinate to the development of its own consultants and the meeting of client needs may fail to achieve these benefits. Some firms, for example, offer little more than a shared name and office space. Others, where profit is over-emphasized, may hire the wrong people, exploit them, subordinate them or foster dependency, or fail to provide sound mentoring. Some firms contractually penalize people severely if they leave the firm, implying that it is not the firm's responsibility to elicit loyalty, but rather its option to force it. Others restrict opportunities for sharing ownership, leadership, and inclusion. Ironically, such practices may force people to react to organizational problems by leaving or by staying and sacrificing self-respect. What a way to educate an organizational consultant!

The consulting firm defines itself by what it rewards and does not reward, as well as *how* it rewards its people. For example, individual compensation based on client billings rewards client billings and competition between consultants. If it does so in a way that is not in the best interests of the client, or in a way that focuses the consultant away from core organizational values or personal or collegial development, then the firm should at least not be surprised by client complaints or by its own lack of organizational unity. Consulting firms have an opportunity to differentiate themselves by the degree to which there is mutual respect and tolerance of individual differences. Professional firm members tend to be particularly demanding and often judgmental toward each other based upon presumed professional skill, billings, success in attracting clients, and other contributions to the firm. Perhaps the tendency for clients to give professionals a lot of respect—sometimes unqualified—leads the professionals to take themselves and their perspectives too seriously, or to overgeneralize about their realms of expertise. *Inter*generationally, there is a temptation to seek to create clones rather than to nurture uniqueness—an everpresent possibility when there are masters and apprentices. The tension between the need to pass on a vision of quality and the need to foster respect and autonomy is never fully resolvable, but those firms that embrace this tension with generosity, openness, and flexibility have a leg up! The further possibility of intragenerational disrespect is best diminished through honest communication and a culture that nurtures the sharing of vulnerability.

To my mind, the ideal to work toward is an organization that selects people who fit well and that manages those people with a consistent focus on enabling them to be congruent and well-aligned within themselves. Such an organization not only fosters its people's development, but through it enables them to intimately comprehend the interactive process that makes it so. It is this vision of human development through organizational catalysis that the consultant is then better equipped —to share, to help managers care.

Epilogue

Yes, but what exactly do
management psychologists really do?

The greatest satisfactions in psychological consulting tend to take years to accrue. For me, the most enduring satisfactions have come in two ways. First, it has been very rewarding to see an organization become more psychologically minded, to *naturally* consider the ripples of cause and effect with people as actions are taken, to see people increasingly focusing on their own development and on stimulating the development of others, and to see these widened perspectives sustained within an organizational culture that passes them on from generation to generation. Inevitably, when this happens, there is also greater congruence between corporate action and personal values.

A second great source of satisfaction for me has come from seeing an individual grow through personal barriers and learn better to optimize his or her effectiveness personally and vocationally. Occasionally, there comes a time when that individual is in a unique position to tackle a particular organizational challenge. Having such a person on board and *ready* at the right time and place can be the difference between the success or failure of a mission. If the mission is critical enough, the person's readiness may well repay the organization for a significant portion of its previous human development investment.

My greatest disappointment came in seeing a client organization with a rich culture and sense of reciprocity unravel when a new president took over. He failed to appreciate the intangible value of his company's flourishing human ecosystem and, in three years, spoiled it. It was no real consolation that this spoilage had been predictable when the new president, upon first being introduced to me, dismissed me with the words, "Nothing personal, but I don't believe in consultants." Eventually, he left, but only after losing or firing most of the people who held the culture together while it thrived, and only after serious financial losses threatened the company's very existence. The synergy within that system—which I had worked so hard to help evolve—had largely faded away. I do take a certain solace in the fact that many people who left have told me that they "took the culture with them" as part of themselves, their values, and their styles. They are shaping their new organizations and the influence continues.

When people ask me what "exactly" it is that I do as a psychologist, I often find myself groping feebly for some way to link my own experience of what I do to that of the questioner. If I simply describe my behavior, it seems too simple. If I describe what I attempt to accomplish, it seems too ephemeral. If I give an example, it is too particular.

How do you explain to people that what you do is sometimes not to give straight answers so as to be helpful? How do you explain that you listen to each person's uniqueness with a "third ear," that you try to understand the person "inside out," and that your response is not programmatic but elicited by what seems to stand out? One finds oneself wanting to say, "Well, you have to *be* there to understand."

In my own learning, I had the fortune, and the frustration, of trying to make sense out of such ambiguous questions twice before in my career—first in learning to be a psychotherapist and second in learning to consult. Since the terrain defined itself mostly in the walking of it, one had to proceed with a great sense of vulnerability at one's blindness—only to discover later that the vulnerability and blindness were more inherent in the task than they were the consequence of inexperience. It amazes me each time I relearn the idea that experience often simply amounts to an acquired comfort with not knowing, and that knowledge and training often contribute little more to the psychologist's performance than does the net to the trapeze artist.

A manager once said it to me this way: "Now that I'm a vice-president, for the first time in my career, there's nothing in my *in box*."

As I write this book—and this is my first book—I ask myself, "Yes, but what exactly do authors really do?"

Appendix A*

What to Evaluate in Psychological Studies[1]

The following questions are intended to stimulate reflection about the characteristics of an individual with whom a psychological study is done.

Intellectual Characteristics

What is the person's basic intellectual capacity or intellectual level? How would you rate her ability to think logically, analytically, and comprehensively in both concrete and abstract areas? Are there any noteworthy differences among specific kinds of intelligence? Does she have any special strengths or weaknesses in dealing with certain kinds of problems? How is the individual's vocabulary and capacity for command of language? How is her nonverbal or quantitative reasoning ability? Is she particularly well equipped to handle technical problems, interpersonal abstractions, spatial relationships?

---

*This section is a substantial revision of original unpublished material by Dr. Edward M. Glaser. I am indebted to him for his graciousness in granting me permission for publication and full freedom to revise. I have also borrowed heavily from the unpublished ideas of J. Watson Wilson and Daniel G. Tear. Naturally, I accept full responsibility for any defects herein.

Is the individual's intellectual effectiveness markedly influenced by emotional factors? Can he maintain concentration under pressure? Is he so afraid of intellectual risk as to become constricted or inhibited intellectually? Does he work up to his intellectual potentials or does he underachieve relative to his potentials? If there is underachievement, is it confined to certain types of problems or is it a more pervasive characteristic?

What are the person's characteristic patterns or styles of problem-solving? Is she chiefly analytical or intuitive, tender-minded or tough-minded? Is her thinking ponderous, methodical, bold, inspirational, conventional, traditional, etc.? Is she an abstract thinker, or does she prefer concrete, tangible problems? Does she work speedily or slowly? Does she tend to guess or work with precision?

Does the individual possess sufficient intellectual discipline? Is he able to be systematic, attentive to detail, organized, and careful when necessary? If so, does he tend to be too detail oriented, too narrow, or too cautious, double- and triple-checking each solution before committing to it even when precision is unwarranted? Or does the person exhibit a scattered or random search until a correct solution is found? Does he tend to give up on a problem after initial failure? Can he correct and re-orient after a false start? Does he go off on tangents?

Does she tend to exercise forethought and good judgment or to ask first and think later? Can she think on her feet? Can she move by inference from problem to solution without having to carefully check every single step in the process? Does she tend to get caught off guard? Can she vary her approach in dealing with different problems?

Does the individual have a cultivated sense of discrimination? Can she distinguish between what is necessary and unnecessary, and between what is important and unimportant? Is she able to reduce complicated subjects, proposals, or discussions to their simplest terms? Can she separate major issues from minor issues?

Does he plan in practical and concrete terms in order to translate broad visions into attainable goals? Can he structure his ideas and plans or does he require external structure? Does he manifest good judgment and level-headedness? Can he apply knowledge in a realistic and practical way? Does he have the facility to move from ideas to decision to appropriate actions and deeds?

Is she able to make competent decisions in the face of conflicting pressures? Can she face and deal with problems without excessive putting-off? Does she need extra time to resolve issues? Is she bold enough to proceed before all the data are in? Does she think with efficiency and focus?

Does the individual have the ability to work with ideas and the relationships among ideas? Does she have facility in assembling a group of seemingly unrelated facts and finding out how they are connected? Does she have overall grasp and breadth—the ability to see the broad picture, to tie things together, and to see relationships? Can she see ramifications beyond immediate concerns? Can she grasp problems outside her special field?

Does the person have a vigorously probing mind, a reflective and natural intellectual curiosity, and a spectrum of interests and knowledge? Does he stay well informed of developments in his field and other fields? Is he receptive to new ideas? Does he passively respond to problems that come his way, or does he look for and become interested in taking the intellectual initiative?

Does the person have a creative imagination? Can she dream and "paint with a big brush"? Can she visualize bigger things than can actually be brought about—and exert constant intellectual effort toward those things? Does she have originality and freshness of thinking? Can she get beyond what is commonly accepted or customary? Will she cross-fertilize her ideas with associates and respond to intellectual give-and-take?

Is the person fluid, alert, and resourceful? Can he find his way around intellectual barriers and reframe questions so they can yield answers? Can the person juggle several balls in the air at once or think on his feet when an obstacle is encountered? Is he observant, inquisitive, and oriented toward scanning for new information?

Is the individual's thinking generally objective—flexibly open to the weight of evidence and to reality factors, rather than distorted by personal prejudices, intellectual rigidity, stereotyping, opinionatedness, stubbornness, personality defenses, and private fantasies? Can she listen to the alternatives provided by others and weigh them judiciously? Can she keep emotional or personal interests from unduly influencing her judgment?

Can she tolerate ambiguity and discriminate among shades of gray, or does she see the world only in black and white terms? Can she appreciate divergent realities? Can she go beyond the immediate facts, or does she tend to oversimplify? Can she see contrasts and make fine distinctions?

Is he characterized by intellectual integrity? Is he able to be constructively self-critical? Does he have the intellectual honesty, independence, and the courage to stick to a decision? Is his thinking characterized by firmness of conviction?

Does she reasonably recognize and accept her approximate level of intellectual capacity? Does she overreach or under-achieve relative to her potential, and is she unduly surprised by the results of her efforts? Does she have the ability to turn experience into an asset, to extract from an experience its full implications?

In summary, the fundamental questions are: What is his *degree* of fundamental intellectual capacity? What *kinds* of intellectual ability does he have? How does he *use* that ability?

Emotional Characteristics

What are the person's characteristic and pervasive traits? How does he feel about himself and his world? Does he tend to be calm and relaxed or nervous and tense? Is he generally good-humored or dyspeptic? Is he even-tempered or mercurial? Do his mood swings result from inner stimuli or outer stimuli? Is he optimistic or pessimistic? Is he carefree or taciturn?

Is she reasonably free from excessive anxieties, worries, obsessions, illusions, fears, guilt feelings, hostility, and neurotic or psychosomatic symptoms? Does she tend to be open and forthright or cautiously reserved? Does she internalize inner feelings and tensions or externalize through spontaneous expression or action?

To what degree is he free of personal ego-hunger and defensiveness? Is he undersensitive or hypersensitive? Will he freely admit mistakes? Does he take himself too seriously or not seriously enough? Can he compete without always having to win; is he able to achieve *and* relax, to work *and* play? Does he sacrifice means for ends or ends for means? Can he tolerate stress and remain poised under pressure? Can he take criticism, rejection, frustration, delay, boredom, and fatigue in reasonable stride, roll with the punches, and still rally to take the initiative and carry on? Is he conceited, apprehensive, self-conscious, or self-deprecating?

What is her level of energy and vitality? Is she active and zestful or sluggish and complacent? Does she have a basic urge to get things done? Is she able to use most of her endowments and to acquire skills that work, or does she tend to fritter away time and energy in emotional self-restriction, poor self-discipline, excessive self-consciousness, or inadequate sense of proportion and perspective? Is she mainly inner-directed or outer-directed, structure-seeking or structure-making? Does she strive toward mastery and seek challenges?

To what degree is the person generally objective and reasonably free from personal ego fragility as contrasted with having many touchy areas, blind spots, illogical hatreds, fanciful ideals, or strong prejudices? Is he suspicious or distrustful, skeptical or cynical? Does he evidence the ability to be reasonable without intellectualizing, to think and to do?

To what extent is the person mature emotionally? Is she weaned, independent, and secure? Is she in touch with her feelings and able to manage them? To what extent is she free from self-absorption, self-deprecation, and overconcern with self-gratification and, therefore, able to focus constructively on facing the demands and challenges of life? Does she evidence the ability to stand out as well as to stand back, to self-scrutinize without being self-absorbed, to be proud and to be humble, to take herself seriously and to laugh at herself, to want to be *her* best without having to be *the* best?

How strong is the person's sense of self? Does he accept himself, berate himself, or ignore himself? Is he conscious of his inner dialogue, and in what tone of voice does this dialogue take place? How strong is his ego and self-concept?

To what degree is she able to demonstrate a persistent willingness to spend time in accomplishing a task, to plod patiently when the load is heavy and the road is steep? Can she attack a problem aggressively? Can she back off? Can she delay gratification? Can she maintain self-discipline?

How easy or difficult is it for him to shift his ideational, motor, or attitudinal sets from one task to another without losing efficiency? Does he have a well-developed sense of the importance of timing? Does he have a sense of perspective, proportion, and priority? Can he adjust rapidly to changing situations; can he cope with the unexpected? Can he handle rejection and loss? Can he leave well enough alone? Is he aware of immediate realities and their implications, and can he grapple with them in a forthright, feet-on-the-ground manner?

What are the person's characteristic styles of adjustment in the face of barriers and obstacles? What are her "fears and fires?" How does she handle frustration? Is she characteristically an action-taker who accepts accountability and tries to pave her fate or a passive, avoidant, perpetual victim of circumstance?

Does he evidence the ability to control and to accept control, to lead and to follow, to take action and to tolerate inaction, to be both passive and active when appropriate? Does he tend to be cautious and wait for the "safe bets," or does he have a well-developed sense of adventure and, if so, in what ways? Is there a confident readiness to take calculated risks for desired objectives?

Does she have the ability to operate within bounds, to expand her horizons, to inhibit and to express? Does she tend to seek an easy life devoid of challenge—a comfortable rut— or does she have a strong will to do and does she seek fulfillment through doing things that require courage, patience, or concentrated effort? What kinds of standards and tolerance does she have for herself and others? Does she set high standards and maintain a strong drive for achievement and accomplishment? Is she active and striving? Does she feel confident with regard to the major areas of living?

Does he evidence the ability to balance self-interest and personal ethics, to navigate through waters of moral ambiguity with both consistency and flexibility? Does he appreciate moral complexity? What are the lines along which he has decided or feels impelled to live his life? What does he stand against and for in his life? What does he seek to be, to become, or to do in life? For what will he make a sacrifice?

Are her goals in line with her long-term needs? What are the essentials for her? What are her choices and emphases when faced with options? What is her guiding emotional core? Is she guided by an overriding value system, and is there congruence among her feelings, thoughts, goals, actions, and values? Can she articulate her value system?

Does the individual have patience, devotion of interest, and determination? Does the person have the ability to idealize without having to be perfect, to find a use for order and for chaos, to focus in and focus out, to structure without obsession, to wander with purpose? Is there a balance between the person's conscience, intellect, and motives?

Does he have personal integrity and ethical intent? Is he of sound character and characterized by a sound personal philosophy of constructive fundamental principles? Does he have a well-developed conscience and sense of obligation? What does he do about the responsibilities with which he is entrusted? How far does he see his responsibilities extending from himself?

Is the person emotionally flexible enough to modify her own attitudes in order to meet the needs of others? Does she have true humility? Can she both give and receive? Can she depend on herself as well as on others, to join and to be alone, to stand on her own two feet and to hold hands?

Can he accept authority without rebelliousness or resentment? Does he experience feelings of alienation from others, or common roots, purposes, and rhythms? Can he forgive and accept forgiveness? Does he have the ability to conform or synchronize in a manner that affirms the self, to nurture his own inner light and those of others, to be frank and to be tactful? Can he be vulnerable with others and give and accept intimacy? Does he feel connected with others and with the world, or does he experience loneliness and alienation?

Does she have zest for life, spontaneity, a creative thrust, and a growing edge? Does she have the ability to refresh her mind and spirit, to feel satisfied, to find sources of strength and renewal for her own spirits? Can she keep an eye on the distant star—to lift her gaze toward the larger purposes of life? Can she transcend daily concerns and her own finite boundaries with a leap of faith? Does she possess a will that is good toward herself, toward others, toward life, and toward living? Does she foster this will in others?

Motivational Characteristics

What is the person's degree of drive? What basic needs seem to move the person? Are these needs external or internal? How does the individual express these needs in behavior? Are there strong peaks and valleys among needs, possibly reflecting greater drive or compulsive insatiability? Or, are the person's needs fairly level, possibly reflecting a blandness of drive or ambivalence characteristic of adolescents? Is the need strong because it reflects conflicts and fantasies of childhood; and if so, has the individual learned to set mature and attainable goals to meet those needs? Are the needs so low as to suggest unconscious rejection of the need; and if so, does the need nevertheless drive the person's actions indirectly?

Does the person evidence a strong need for affectionate and intimate relationships with others and for deep emotional attachment? Is there an unbounded craving for acceptance and an insecurity about rejection? Does he constantly need reassurance or is he able to do some self-prodding? If his need for affection is low, does it mean that he values cooler distance, or is he afraid of emotional entanglements? If it is high, does the need lead to hypersensitivity; and if low, does it lead to insensitivity?

To what extent is the individual motivated by the need to operate interdependently, to achieve a sense of belonging, to join, to be a partner, or to follow? If the need is high, is it an indication of healthy mutuality or immature dependency? On the other hand, is there a need not to have to rely upon others? If so, does it lead to a healthy capacity to operate independently or to an inability to truly join, to appreciate boundaries, to ask for help when it is necessary, or to work in tandem with others?

To what extent does the person seek restriction and boundedness? Does she prefer the calculated risk, security, harmony, balance, stability, and predictability? If so, does this reflect insecurity and lead to rigidity, passivity, immobility, emotional blandness, and a failure to stretch potentials? Is she afraid to "rock the boat"? On the other hand, does she seek expansion and resist boundaries? Does she look for diversity, change, unlimited possibilities, and freedom and spontaneity of action and expression? If so, can she accept reasonable boundaries, work within structures, and tolerate rules and guidelines? Or, is there evidence of impulsivity, constant impatience, and a refusal to be guided by tradition or rules of the game? Will the person create turmoil for its own sake?

Is the individual oriented toward power, persuasion, authority, influence, and impact? Does it lead to a willingness to take on authority, to take charge, to make things happen, and to be where the action is? Does it lead her to be prime moving, assertive, forceful, and dominant? Or, does it reflect a desire to make sure that she is not "bossed" by others, a reaction to felt impotence, a fear of vulnerability, or the acting out of fantasies of omnipotence? Does it lead to authoritarian, domineering, overcontrolling, or intimidating approaches to others or to situations? Or, does she prefer not to lead; but, instead, to let others make the decisions and take responsibility for actions? Does this reflect a contentment with going with the flow; or does it reflect deeper passivity, a fatalistic attitude, or passive aggressiveness?

Does the person gain satisfaction from the use of logic,

reason, theory, or creativity? Are these a means of self-expression and goal-attainment? Does this lead him to be easily stimulated by intellectual challenges and to test his intellectual limits? Does it reflect an inability to accept the value of emotions; and, does it lead to overrationality, to analyzing but not solving, to thinking but not acting, to insisting on facts but denying intuitions? Does he, on the other hand, stress a practical and down-to-earth approach with less emphasis upon theoretical or abstract issues? If so, does this reflect insecurity regarding his intellectual adequacy, an avoidance of rationality or intellectual expression, or a lack of intellectual discipline?

Does the person evidence a need to behave in a determined, tenacious, and persistent fashion, to use willpower as an end as well as a means toward an end? Does this lead her to be highly self-disciplined, dutiful, and steadfast, or does it lead her to wear blinders, to be stubborn, or dogmatic, to fail to take perspective and to anticipate adversity? Does she practice denial or assume that wishing makes it so? On the other hand, is she more prone toward flexibility regarding persistence and duty, more oriented toward shifting gears and finding shortcuts and short-lived enthusiasms? If so, to what degree can she nevertheless muster discipline when necessary, or does she make excuses for not trying or for not "keeping the plow in the ground"? Is she willing to make the effort and the sacrifices that are required to attain life goals?

To what extent does the individual have a need to exploit opportunities, to seize the advantage, to partake in the interplay of the marketplace, to react resourcefully to incoming stimuli, to venture, and to risk? If this need is high, can the person resist distraction and keep a focus on long-term goals and ethical congruence? Can he temper self-interest and short-term gain for broader purposes? Does he require stimulation in order to react? On the other hand, is he less inclined to react to opportunity, more selective regarding goals, characterized by greater uniformity of pace? If so, does he fail to notice opportunity and wonder why others "get all the breaks"? Does he fear exploitation and react with characteristic counterexploitiveness?

Does the individual evidence a need for social recognition, respect, status, prestige, and a sense of communality with others? Does this lead her to maintain a conforming, poised, and diplomatic stature and to exhibit a strong sense of communal obligation and commitment? Or, does it reflect shallowness and social insecurity and lead to superficiality, pretentiousness, stressing appearance over substance, or intolerance for divergence? On the other hand, is she more inclined toward nonconformity, less of a joiner, and less inclined to identify with the majority, and more individualistic? If so, does this reflect a healthy willingness to question tradition and a preference for following her own inner light; or, does it reflect adolescent nonconformity, a fear of being unacceptable to others, a compensatory "I don't care what others think" attitude, an inability to fit in, an insensitivity to social expectations, or a perpetual rebellion against "the establishment," or a task focus without a people focus?

Does the individual evidence a strong need to be his "personal best," to engage in activities that reflect well upon him, bring out the best in him, and lead to pride of accomplishment? If so, is he self-scrutinizing, self-demanding, and selective about the goals he chooses? Does he have to be in the spotlight all the time? Is there evidence of narcissistic self-absorption, grandiosity, emphasis on appearances, selfishness, or an inability to sustain momentum when there is no opportunity to shine? Is the preoccupation on looking good rather than accomplishing, on the process rather than the result? Is the person too selective regarding goals? On the other hand, does he prefer to operate behind the scenes, to emphasize characteristics of modesty and humility, to do what needs to be done without concern for issues of pride or grandeur? If so, is there an underlying lack of sense of self or pride in self, a fear of introspection, a denial of selfhood?

Does the individual show a strong need for competitive achievement, for winning, for acquiring, and for building? Does it lead her to attempt to climb the ladder of success based on a long-term game plan? Does it lead to workaholism, over-competitiveness, or an inability to accept defeat? On the other hand, does she tend to deemphasize competitiveness and acquisitiveness? Can she, nevertheless, compete when in competition; or, is she inclined to underachieve, to fear competition, or to live only for the day?

Does the person evidence a strong need for autonomy and self-sufficiency? Is it important for him to be self-directing and self-stimulating, to work on his own or by himself; and, does this lead him to venture out, to explore his potentials, and to fend for himself? Does it lead him to be insular, to fear intimacy, to have to do everything alone? On the other hand, does he show a need to be around others and not to maintain independence? If so, does it lead him to be harmonizing and conventional? Or does it reflect a deeper fear of being alone or abandoned? Is he paralyzed when called upon to strike out on his own?

Does the individual evidence a strong need for order, attention to detail, structure, and accuracy? If so, does it lead to analytical depth, punctuality, and elegance of craftsmanship? Or, does it lead to obsessiveness, narrowness, and picayune excursions? Or, does she, instead, stress spontaneity, breadth, and creative chaos? Does she, therefore, welcome ambiguity, play with possibility, and enjoy the unexpected? If so, can the individual keep track of details, stay within bounds, and stay on track?

Insight Into One's Self and Into Others

To what degree is the person aware of the roots and background forces that have shaped his style of life? Is his awareness only at a descriptive level; or, does he understand the major dynamic forces which have tended to shape his development? Does his self-concept reflect perspective and objectivity? Is he aware of his own tendencies, characteristics, potentials, limitations, strengths, and shortcomings? Is he more self-critical than self-analytical? Does he have a good grasp of his inner needs, and are the goals he sets to meet those needs typically well chosen? Has he chosen a realistic and appropriate level of aspiration? Is his self-image consistent with the way others would see him, and is he aware of his own impact on others? Does he often get surprised at others' behavior or attitudes? Does he even think about these kinds of things?

Does the person practice internal vigilance as a means of self-improvement on a continuing basis? Is she characterized by sufficient self-accountability, flexibility, and psychological-mindedness to be able to use experience in the service of constructive change? What are the blind spots or areas of subjectivity that skew or distort her view of reality in particular directions? Is she prone toward self-justification, rationalization, hyperbole, minimization, or extremes of thought? Is there evidence of projection, repression, or other defensive barriers to fluid insight development? Is the individual reasonably in touch with her own feelings? Can she constructively use internal as well as external data, logical as well as nonlogical data, and verbal as well as nonverbal data? Is she capable of exhibiting a sense of humor about her own foibles and shortcomings as well as those of others?

To what degree and in what way does the person understand or evaluate other people and their reactions? Does he make the effort? Can he sense unstated attitudes, feelings, and motives? Can he distinguish between sincerity and bluff? Are there consistent biases in his assessment of others? Is he aware of individual differences? Does he attempt to make differentiations; or, does he tend only to see others at a surface level? Does he have the ability to observe and interpret minimal cues in dealing with people? Does he see the people-component in issues? Can he sense the climate or morale of a group? Is he perceptive, penetrating, sensitive, and/or empathic? Is he able to understand the underlying motives of others? Is he tolerant or intolerant of the weaknesses of others? Does he gloss over negatives or over-emphasize them? Is he able to see through others' eyes and listen through others' ears and, thus, appreciate why people feel and act as they do? Does he have appreciation and respect for divergent realities, perspectives, world views, and values?

How does the individual use the insights she develops? Is she active or passive regarding insights? Does she use insights to accommodate, to adapt, to manipulate, to help, to rescue, or to control others? Does she evidence skill in balancing the feelings, needs, and ideas of others with her own? Does she have skill in resolving discrepancies of meaning in the communication process? Can she judge when to react to the "facts," and when to search for hidden agenda?

Interpersonal Characteristics

Does the person maintain a pleasant, agreeable, and friendly manner when meeting people? Is he interested in people? Is he introverted and solitary or extroverted and gregarious? Is he well-mannered, poised, and reasonably free of annoying mannerisms, ostentatiousness, approval-seeking behavior, or pretentiousness? How would you characterize his general social impact, and how well does he wear over time? To what extent does he exhibit the characteristic of stature or presence with others? Does he tend to blend in or to stand out, to lead or to follow, to participate or to withdraw? Is he relatively consistent in ideas, attitudes, and behavior; or, is there a good deal of variance, depending upon time, circumstances, or moods? Is he articulate and skilled in oral expression? Is he able to carry on a conversation, to put ideas across, to stay on the point, and to convey what he means? Can he dramatize an issue to bring it alive?

Does the individual typically exhibit good will toward others and toward life? Does she generally facilitate or hinder group action in accomplishing a group task? Is she characteristically kind and gracious to people when there is no special need? Is there generosity in her assumptions about the intents of others? Does she give others the benefit of the doubt?

Does she exhibit a spirit of compromise and acceptance of the habits, tastes, and preferences of others? Does she convey amicability, appreciation, humility, and receptiveness with others? Can she adjust to different types of people as they are, not as she would like them to be? Does she overreact to or withdraw from certain types of people or to people in general? Does she tend to adopt a cordial and affirming attitude toward others, or one that is aloof and hostile? Is she forgiving or vengeful? Is she oriented toward or away from acceptance and a spirit of accommodation? Is she capable of both experiencing and conveying genuine respect toward others? Does she tend to be more cooperative or competitive, warm or cool, straightforward or circumventive, selfish or unselfish, fair-minded or biased, passive or active, trusting or suspicious, and, honest or deceptive? Is she considerate, helpful, thoughtful, gracious, and able to restrain her personal impulses and desires out of consideration for others? Is there evidence of arrogance, crudeness, self-righteousness, sarcasm, self-consciousness, obsequiousness, posturing, hostility, stiffness, deviousness, insincerity, or manipulativeness? Does she put a high value on another person's time? Does she give people a sense of being in a hurry, or is she generally relaxed and available to others? Does she readily like people for themselves, or does she use people as an audience or for personal gain? To which kinds of people is she likely to feel closest or least close?

Does the person inspire the confidence of others? To what extent is he characterized by directness, aggressiveness, assertiveness, energy, persuasiveness, and a willingness to take the lead or the social initiative? Can he be adequately forceful in dealing with unpleasant situations? Can he balance diplomacy, discretion, and tact with frankness and confrontation? What are the differences, if any, in the way he treats subordinates, associates, and superiors? Can he respect the ideas and performance of people whom he dislikes personally? Can he energize others? Can he understand and elicit the best from people who are of lower social status, educational attainment, or intellectual capacity? Can he facilitate the attainment of group objectives?

Does the individual evidence simple sincerity and searching honesty? Is she a good listener? Does she know when to talk and when to listen? Does she listen with a sincere desire to understand and to make the best use of another person's point of view? Does she generally have a good sense of humor, including the ability to laugh at herself? Is she generally good humored or humorless? Does she have a sense of fun, of shared play? Can she truly share and truly join with others? Can she give to others as well as take from others with comfort and naturalness? Has she developed the skill of concomitantly affirming the self and others? Can she forgive past hurts and deal with relationships in the present?

To what extent does this individual exhibit the traits, characteristics, and behaviors common to a particular culture, nationality, geographical region, subculture, socioeconomic class, or ethnic, linguistic, or racial group? Does he exhibit these characteristics with comfort and ease or is there some awkwardness in his outward expression of his self-identity? Can he adapt his behavior to those who fall into other groups and accommodate divergent characteristics with grace? Is he comfortable dealing with others across generational lines? Does he have a willingness to explore cross-cultural differences?

Vocational Characteristics

How do the characteristics of the person "come together" in his approach to his job? What are his vocational and career interests and ambitions? How does he go about applying the relevant "technology" of his job? If the job is selling, how does he sell? If the job is managing, how does he manage? If the job is basket weaving, how does he weave baskets? What is the person's ability to initiate, plan, organize, and direct action? Does he typically develop and use a plan? If so, is the plan tactical, strategic, or a combination of both? Is he capable of broad planning, or does he just focus on specific issues or details? Is he able to plan a steady work flow? Is he better as a visionary, implementor, or follower? Can he distinguish between small and great matters for decisions and teach others to do the same? Can he shift fluidly from abstract to concrete and back? Can he focus on the target without losing sight of the details of implementation? Does he characteristically seek and envision better ways of doing things; and, is he resourceful enough to find the means of putting these ideas into practice? Does he see and act upon new opportunities? Does he move ahead reactively or according to well-defined principles or concepts? Is he objective in weighing evidence for or against proposed courses of action?

How determined is the individual to accomplish personal objectives? To what degree does she summon energy, drive, and perseverance toward the attainment of goals? Can she endure long periods without success? Is she one who makes things happen, who takes charge, who is willing to rock the boat, who can be an effective prime mover? Is she prompt to take hold of a problem? What is her degree of drive and ingenuity in finding means to achieve ends? Will she characteristically work up to her highest potential? Does she put first things first, or tend to "grease the wheel that squeaks the loudest," or to procrastinate in getting to the less enjoyable portions of the work? Does she use time effectively? Is she more effective at following through on a specific job, organizing a system, or supervising complex organizational details? Or, is she more of a promoter or an "idea person," but disinterested or weak on the follow-through? What are her standards of accuracy and thoroughness? Does she have the capacity to run things—to take responsibility—and to manage things in a well-organized way that makes for superior accomplishment or end results? Does she have a good understanding of the operating mechanism of a business? Does she know how to apply management principles at many levels? Can she handle many pressing problems in rapid-fire order? Can she tolerate constant interruption? Can she retain many problems in mind simultaneously and juggle priorities for action?

Can the person feel like an integral part of an organization, and, if so, under what circumstances? Can he identify with the organization to the degree that a powerful motivation and source of satisfaction stems from organizational success or business development? Does he give time, effort, and devotion to becoming more and more adept at a job, and what are the conditions which best bring out this behavior? Does he possess a comprehensive philosophy of management and a sensitivity to the problems of building a spirited and effective team of people? Is he able to think from an organizational point of view and, yet, be loyal to subordinates—accepting full accountability for their actions—as well as to superiors and to his own conscience? Can he compromise without being or feeling compromised?

Does the individual tend to view superiors as a guiding or consulting source, or as an inhibiting force? Are her attitudes toward authority potential sources of organizational conflict? Does she work best under freedom and responsibility for operation in an unstructured or semi-structured pattern; or does she require a structured situation in which standard practice can be followed? Will the stimulus of greater responsibility or of greater demand set by a superior help to motivate her, or is it best to allow her to proceed at her own pace?

Does the person set a sound example of effective leadership? Is he able to inspire loyalty and to work cooperatively and respectfully with people at all levels of the organization? Can he motivate others to full effectiveness? Is he a good teacher, coach, and assessor of people? What is his ability to select, train, and develop subordinates, to assign them suitably, and to keep track of their performance? Does he generally maintain an attitude of trust and approval in dealing with subordinates and associates, even though realistically recognizing their characteristics, tendencies, or limitations? Does he expect others to pace themselves at his rate; or, does he evidence sensitivity to and respect for other people's rates, styles, or energy levels? Can he effectively represent and transmit the values and priorities that guide the organization to his subordinates? Is he willing and able to be responsive to the expectations handed down from superiors?

Does the individual keep people properly informed of matters which affect them? Can, and will, she generally make clear the reasons behind her actions? Can she effectively delegate responsibilities and commensurate authority, or does she overcontrol or underinvolve others? Does she avoid going around people or over people's heads? Is she willing to encourage participation on the part of subordinates, and is she skillful in tapping the creative ideas of others? Does she solicit new ideas in order to improve methods and procedures? Does she play a catalytic role as a supervisor? Is she vitally interested in the people around her? Does she have a genuine interest in the training and development of subordinates?

How does the person try to lead? What is the individual's characteristic management style: easy-going, benevolent, stern, clear, fair, dynamic inspirational, demanding, firm, visionary, conservative, rigid, risk-avoidant, challenging, systematic, or authoritarian? Will he err on the lenient side? Can he make hard people decisions, and in what time frame, and with what skill? Does he supervise by authority, suggestions, personal enthusiasm, explanation, example, or by invitation to group problem solving? Will he hold people accountable for their actions or overprotect them? In what areas, with what problems, or in what environment is he most and least effective? What would he need to remember about his own error tendencies in order to maximize effectiveness over the long-haul? What can his manager do to bring out his best potentials on an ongoing basis, to help him feel empowered to stretch, and to help him avoid the probable pitfalls of his style?

What particular issues need to be considered in managing this individual in a manner that will meet her needs, promote her growth, and foster her effectiveness? How easy is she to manage? Does she need structure, challenge, incentives, praise, applause, reassurance, concrete directions, absence of risk, clear feedback, a safe and predictable environment, a close working relationship, intellectual stimulation, freedom and latitude, prodding, redirection from blind alleys, deadlines, time to think, support in dealing with other departments, or something else? How will she react if what is needed is unavailable? How will she react when there are setbacks, crises, temptations, losses, failures, or disappointments? How will she deal with risk, uncertainty, rejection, lack of control, or unfairness in others?

---

1. *What to evaluate in psychological studies,* by Lester L. Tobias, copyright © 1988 by Nordli, Wilson Associates. Reprinted with permission by Nordli, Wilson Associates.

Appendix B

Preface to Psychological Evaluation Report

Psychological Study of ————

This report is intended to be an aid in this person's vocational and personal growth. Only this individual and those in a position to constructively influence the person's development should have access to the report—and only with the individual's consent. The report's contents must be considered in light of other relevant data, and the author should be consulted on the report's proper interpretation and implementation. Safeguard the report by keeping it in a confidential file. Since it has been written for a specific time and place, the report can be understood only in that framework and should be destroyed when no longer timely.

Appendix C
Psychological Studies*

PSYCHOLOGICAL STUDY 1
Product Development Manager, Age 36

Mr. ———— ranks in the top 1 percent of the general population in his current level of intellectual functioning and problem-solving ability. He is, therefore, capable of handling a wide range of complex and abstract problems. He is a reflective and integrative thinker with an inquisitive and deeply probing mind. Drawn toward the complex and abstract, he tends to view ideas as ends in themselves, and focuses more on the theoretical than the strictly practical, down to earth, or concrete. As a visionary who looks beyond and ahead of the immediate facts, he can sometimes fail to see that which is immediate, concrete, and relevant, leading others occasionally to perceive his thinking as "in the clouds," "flaky," too philosophical, or insufficiently pragmatic. Similarly, he has a subtle appreciation for complexity and can approach problems with depth and richness of analysis—a characteristic that can prevent him from being maximally decisive, incisive, and constructively simple.

---

*The psychological studies presented here are all fictitious. Any similarity to any person, living or dead, or to any existing psychological study report, is pure coincidence.

143

More rational and logical than intuitive, he is inclined to see data as "hard facts." Therefore, he can sometimes fail to consider the effects of his ideas on others or alternatives provided by others when the alternative position is built upon a less-elegant intellectual foundation than his own. He has the courage of his convictions and is not afraid to take a controversial position. In fact, he can be stubborn on occasion and somewhat relentless in his use of logic, and this relentlessness can restrict his breadth of vision. Yet, he is not usually narrow and can deal with interpretational ambiguity.

He falls within the normal ranges of emotional stability. He experiences a kind of rootless alienation, a tendency to feel different from others, to feel that he does not quite fit in, to feel out of step with his interpersonal environment. In compensation, he has developed a very individualistic adjustment, emphasizing a very strongly felt need to be different and unique, to be self-reliant, and to define his path in a self-contained and even idiosyncratic manner. He is resistive and oppositional if forced to fit a mold. He has developed confidence in his ability to sustain his efforts, to accept challenge, and to test his intelligence, although deep down he lacks self-acceptance and tends to experience more strain than the average person.

In an effort to compensate for lack of self-acceptance, he works hard to prove himself, but his satisfactions tend to be short-lived or transitory. While often constructive, active, and self-initiating in dealing with barriers, he lacks a full array of mature outlets for stress and tension. Tending to overpersist in the face of barriers, he can fail to anticipate adversity because his overpersistence involves wearing "emotional blinders." He is inclined to emphasize reason over emotion and to see the logical aspects of problems while ignoring the feeling side of life.

His adjustments allow him to keep anxiety contained but can limit his growth as well as his ability to synchronize with others. On the inside, he experiences a taut intensity and a brooding insularity that are juxtaposed with a searching for spiritual quiescence and magnitude of purpose. He is often impelled to reach out and search idealistically, but with a certain inevitability of disappointment. Deep down, he knows what letting go is worth, but he knows, too, the risks and is afraid to jump into uncharted waters. The price he pays, then, is a loss of constructive emotional vulnerability, intimacy, and spontaneity. It leads him to feel alienated, isolated, and apart.

Motivationally, he has a high degree of self-sustaining drive and energy of an internal nature. Intellectual challenges are very stimulating to him, and he goes out of his way to prove himself intellectually, to tackle difficult problems, to maintain a reasonable and logical approach, and to seek out tough or novel solutions. It is very important to him that he be the master of his own destiny, and he is inclined to approach his life with an emphasis on will power, persistence, steadfastness, and self-discipline. His independence is of great importance to him, and he is most comfortable when free from dependence upon others. As indicated above, his uniqueness and individualism are important to him, and he is motivated to operate in a fairly nonconforming, even idiosyncratic, manner.

He enjoys situations in which he can have impact and influence, and likes to be in positions of authority. He is not a highly opportunistic individual and can be fairly singularly focused in his approach in that he is not inclined to be reactive politically or to consider momentary situational advantage. He dislikes feeling bounded, confined, or constrained, and is inclined to test limits. Similarly, while alert to a sense of intellectual order, he dislikes routine or mundane activities.

There is an inconsistency between his intellectual insights into himself and other people and his psychological insights. At an intellectual level, his descriptive insights are often accurate; however, since he errs toward overrationality, his data tend to lack wholeness, depth, and color. Therefore, he fails to appreciate some of the subtleties of behavior, and can lack sensitivity and empathy despite his good intentions. As a result, he has not developed a significant array of deep insights to enable him to differentiate among the characteristics of other people and to address them based on their differences. This reduces his interpersonal effectiveness and leads to rough spots in his relationships. Similarly, with respect to his own growth, while introspective, there is some tendency for him to rationalize his failures and occasionally to fail to face up to the emotional underpinnings of his own behavior. He certainly recognizes his feelings, but he has blind spots as to their source. Sometimes he is surprised by the reactions of others, especially to his own impact. Similarly, he tends to avoid situations he views as "political," since he has difficulty drawing the line between constructive accommodation and deception.

Interpersonally, he is somewhat awkward but very informal and unpretentious. He is inclined to be nonconforming and to present himself as very much his own man. He can be seen by others as mildly contemptuous or pedantic, owing to his high intelligence and emphasis on strict logic. His independence can lead him to be viewed as lacking in team spirit and as a bit of a "prima donna" even though he is basically well intentioned and willing to pitch in. He is basically dependable and reliable. Those willing to overlook his occasional tactlessness and social rough edges can come to see that he is sincere and well-meaning by nature and can find him engaging and stimulating. Dynamic, persuasive, and self-assertive, he is inclined to adopt a "take me as I am" attitude, which can create problems for him with people who are not likely to be tolerant of his foibles. He is frank and sincere but insufficiently constructively incongruent.

Organizationally, he is inclined to be a maverick, to stir things up, and to make waves. He can be a prime mover, likes to take charge, and likes to make things happen. At times, he is a bit of a "bull in a china shop" because of his lack of a sense of organizational politics and lack of diplomacy. Thus, despite his creative ideas and high intelligence, his effectiveness can be reduced by the way he presents his ideas. He can be effective with conceptual issues as well as far-reaching issues, although he needs to work more on being relevant and practical on a day-to-day basis. While he has a strong individual action orientation, he lack managerial sophistication. Only a fairly limited number of people would develop under him—perhaps, for example, very bright, confident, but relatively inexperienced people. Even there, there is the risk that they would learn some poor interpersonal habits.

He works best for a boss who recognizes his talent, provides a flow of stimulation and challenge, and allows him time, latitude, and freedom. His boss could help him by providing very direct feedback on his interpersonal impact, and also by helping others to respect his need to operate without too many constraints. When necessary, he will need to be reminded about his accountability for results and his interpersonal impact. Similarly, at times, he will need some structuring, refocusing, and redirecting, and in order to help him keep his eye on relevant targets and to keep his activity within organizationally consonant bounds.

CONCLUSIONS AND PROGNOSIS

Mr. ———— is not your average anything. His high intelligence certainly sets him apart, and he has cultivated his individuality and uniqueness. He has done so at a price in that he is less able to synchronize with others than the average person, and this leads him to feel more insular and to be less effective in organizational settings. His high intelligence, action orientation, and hard-working conscientiousness do often compensate, but the overall result is one of some inconsistency, and occasionally more heat than light.

As a starting place in his own development, Mr. ———— would find value in working on ways of becoming more self-accepting. This would enable him to be more generous both to himself and to others and would likely increase his tolerance. By opening himself more to others, he would gain in his own appreciation of himself and in his sense of his own potential stature. He would also be likely to experience the acceptance of others to a greater degree. In time he could begin to feel more comfortable with his own and others' feelings and with nonrational values and to feel less need to stay in control through reason. It would also help him to forgive foibles more and to see integrity as more of a continuum than a dichotomy. By facing himself squarely at an emotional level, he could experience his own emotions and his relationships with others more spontaneously and deeply. As he redirects his passions more toward freeing up his own creativity and away from so much emotional control, his own sense of clarity of self will improve. He has the requisite capabilities for further personal development. His further growth will require the courage to encounter his ordinariness.

He would do well to reconsider his place within organizations and to consider working on some of those issues that lead him to encounter rough spots. He might try to push less, to back off more, to survey the scene, and to survey his emotions. He might benefit from reminding himself what his longer-term priorities are when considering whether to take a strong position or to let it go. This may also help him to focus on pragmatic realities. It would be helpful to him to focus on his impact on others, and to reflect on how others perceive him, even when he believes that others are being illogical. It would help him to keep his audiences in mind and to seek feedback from those he trusts. He might want to consider taking courses, seminars, or workshops of an interpersonal nature in order to refine his skills, particularly those that promise a high degree of feedback.

However, ultimately he and his organization might achieve the greatest satisfaction by finding ways to build on his very real potential strengths. Rather than focusing on the development of management skills, for example, he could grow into becoming an effective organizational ombudsman, devil's advocate, and intellectual stimulant—particularly as he develops the insight to face his own human limitations and the faith to rely on his strengths.

PSYCHOLOGICAL STUDY 2
Vice President of Sales and Marketing, Age 51

Ms. ———'s current level of intellectual functioning is in the top 2 percent of the general population. She is, therefore, capable of handling a wide range of quantitative as well as verbal data comprehensively, integratively, and with depth and discernment. A broad thinker with a reflective, philosophical, exploratory, and inquisitive outlook, she is rather flexible and tolerant of ambiguity. She seeks to differentiate subtlety and nuance and is a synthesizer who looks for possibilities. More the visionary and the far-reacher than the short-term decision maker, she is nevertheless often able fluidly to shift focus back to the narrow from her more stylistic broad viewpoint. She is adept at incorporating the ideas of others without losing sight of her convictions. She has the discernment to sort through bias and intellectual camouflage. When she errs, it is on the side of imprecision and lack of concreteness. Her successes often result from her vision.

She is subtly autocritical and concerned with improving the quality of her own thinking. While she has strong convictions, she knows how to listen. Her intellectual integrity is high. She has the temperament for objectivity and practices it as a talent. She is pragmatic and result oriented, but she does have a certain contempt for the mundane, the trivial, and peripheral distractions and details. This contempt can sometimes lead her to be less acutely aware of the eddies and undercurrents that can signal potential adversity. In general, she uses her very high intelligence with an expansive, fluid efficiency.

Emotionally, she is stable and mature. She is spiritually wholesome and has a very well-developed sense of purpose and a well-articulated value system that is highly integrated with her actions. She knows what she stands for and keeps her ideals in the forefront in order to maintain alignment. She is generally in tune with others, maintaining a generous and well-meaning attitude. She is very aware of the need to stretch herself out internally, to self-scrutinize, and she does so with an experienced naturalness.

A confident and expansive individual, she enjoys challenges and sets high standards for herself. She has a strong ego and a sure-footed resiliency in the face of barriers and problems. She is inclined to be overly stoic, controlled, dutiful, serious, and responsible, and this causes her to be more tense, tight, self-conscious, self-constraining, and moody than she needs to be. Perhaps there is a bit more room for "want" in "should" than she realizes; she could, for example, become lighter and more enjoyable to others by allowing herself to be more self-indulgent and less self-inhibiting without sacrificing integrity and congruence.

Her sense of responsibility is extensive and intensive. She has a strong sense of her impact and her accountabilities, and this constellation is central to her motivation. Also, it is deeply important to her that she control her fate, and she enjoys operating with a sense of autonomy, independence, self-directionality, and self-reliance. She fears helplessness but is learning to depend more on others and has come to enjoy the interrelatedness it brings. Yet, when the chips are down, it is herself she calls upon, and her solitary attempts at succor can have its bitter edge. Ideas arouse and impel her; she finds details arid. Competition, materialism, and opportunism are, for her, distractions.

She is introspective, self-aware, and self-analytical. She is usually in touch with her feelings but cautious and self-bounding in expressing them. This steeliness of emotional posture can temper her receptivity to feelings despite her very well-intentioned and basically sensitive nature. She works hard on herself, fine tunes her emotional tools, and is emotionally vigilant. She is, therefore, receptive to criticism and deeply oriented toward personal growth. Her stature reflects her growth.

She is perceptive about individual differences and has developed a large foundation of discerning insights into people's characters and personalities. She is tolerant, but this disposition does not temper the acuteness of her perception. She is, therefore, able to tailor her behavior to the needs of a wide range of people and a wide range of circumstances. She can tend to avoid confrontation, but not for too long. Her self-righteous side can lead her toward occasional dogmatism, but she usually keeps these tendencies in check through her self-honesty and her perspective. Her insights, then, are usually on target and are often rather penetrating.

She is a sincere and honest individual with a good deal of presence, poise, and interpersonal self-command. She is approachable and outgoing, although she is really an introvert. Thus, while capable of warmth, she has her self-conscious and self-inhibiting side, which gives her some measure of reserve or aloofness. People would see her as credible, trustworthy, unselfish, caring, and characterized by integrity. Despite her honesty, leveling does not come easy to her, and the disharmony of confrontation is not her strong suit. When she errs, it is on the side of tact, diplomacy, and discretion. She seeks depth in her relationships, but people can see her as somewhat impenetrable by others.

She is hard-working, determined, tenacious, and career-oriented. She is clearly more conceptual and idealistic than goal-oriented or task-oriented, but her idealism is also pragmatic, and she has a good sense of priorities. Nevertheless, as indicated above, she could benefit from working on attending more to day-to-day details. Her sophistication in managing and developing subordinates and enhancing morale is high. Despite her willingness to delegate and, in fact, her occasional tendency to overdelegate, she knows who is in charge and does not shrink from decisions. She is an effective prime mover who makes her impact felt. She provides a model but is also willing to guide. She leads by expectation, example, and concept. She understands development and applies her skill rather maturely and genuinely. Her character, intelligence, and objectivity are her strongest suits. From these strengths occasionally sprout dogmatism, overreflectivity, and an overly global focus; however, her overall maturity and capacity for self-scrutiny normally keep these tendencies in check. She is, therefore, capable of continuing to make solid and sustaining contributions to the organization.

CONCLUSIONS AND PROGNOSIS

Ms. ——— is a person who has attended well to her own growth, and her stature and impact are significant reflections of this effort. Her character is fertile soil. She has so many potential psychological resources at her disposal that her primary challenge is to continue to build on these resources. She might benefit, for example, from managing her internal controls a bit more loosely, thus allowing herself more spontaneity and vulnerable intimacy, particularly where giving via taking is concerned. While she may need to watch out for the potential for stylistic inflexibility to narrow her options, her strengths serve her well overall.

Her idealism can provide a stimulus to herself and others, but it can also potentially inhibit. Her idealism can be uplifting, but her distaste for the mundane could constrain her pragmatism. Her interpersonal sensitivity and insight can facilitate her leadership of others, but, in conjunction with her natural self-reliance, could inhibit constructive confrontations. For Ms. ———, developmental techniques are unnecessary. Simply building on her insights is the order of the day.

PSYCHOLOGICAL STUDY 3
Materials Manager, Age 42

Mr. ——— is in the top 25 percent of the general population in his current level of intellectual functioning and problem-solving ability. He is at his best when dealing with relatively concrete and structured activities where he can obtain a hands-on feel for the problems he has to solve and where there are fairly well-spelled-out conditions and traditional ways for solving the problems at hand. A step-by-step, level-headed, careful, and deliberate thinker, he likes to look before he leaps in order to be on safe ground before making a decision. He is thorough, accurate, orderly, organized, and perfectionistic, and not one to leave loose ends untied. He prefers operating with relatively tangible and finite challenges as opposed to those that are indefinite, abstract, or continually changing. Thus, he is not highly reflective or creatively visionary; instead, he is more inclined toward steadiness, structuring, and methodical approaches. While he can be decisive when guidelines and rules are clear, he is not an intellectual risk taker.

More adept at factual or black and white issues than with shades of gray or ambiguity, he tends to become frustrated when goals and objectives are not laid out in detail. He is more of a doer than a thinker and, therefore, prefers to act rather than to ponder and conceptualize. Thus, he likes to emphasize practical results that he can see in the here and now. He can exhibit a degree of stubbornness when he is unsure of the context, but, on the other hand, he is relatively compliant when he understands the structure and the guidelines. He is relatively effective in drawing on his native capacities in his day-to-day problem-solving activities and, in this sense, is an extender. He does have to put out a good deal of effort when dealing with complex or abstract issues and can sometimes feel over his head in such areas.

Emotionally, he is stable and well-controlled. He is a rather responsible individual who is loyal to his family and his company. His values are clear and consistently held, and his character is firm. He is very persistent and dedicated in the pursuit of his goals, and he is certainly not a quitter. He is a self-reliant, dutiful, and serious individual.

He is more of a responder than an initiator, more environmentally dependent than self-navigating, so he responds best with structure and context. His self-concept is not as highly developed as it could be and he is not one to look inside himself very deeply. Therefore, he does not always know himself, and this can sometimes lead him to respond somewhat reflexively to outside stimulation.

He is a fairly conservative individual and is more restrictive than expansive in his approach to life. Thus, he places greater value on security, harmony, and balance than on adventure, change, or risk. He is willing to face up to barriers, but he tends to be content with the status quo without outside stimulation. He is quite persistent, once energized, and capable of a good deal of self-discipline. He can, in fact, be stubbornly persistent, overly focused, and inclined toward worry and compulsiveness when situations are not going well for him. As a result, he sometimes fails to anticipate adversity, and he may press forward so intently that he feels he is bashing his head against a brick wall. At such times, it would be helpful for him to learn to relax, to accept himself more, to adjust to his limitations more, and to adopt a more distanced perspective.

He is the kind of individual who likes operating in a predictable, consistent, and structured environment. He seeks a good deal of social support and likes to belong to a team where there are affable relationships and a sense of harmony and esprit de corps. He is not averse to leadership but needs strong leadership from others in order to perform at his best. He is more inclined to systematize than to innovate, and more inclined toward implementation than strategy setting or conceptualization. He is not very ambitious, financially competitive, or entrepreneurial, and tends not to seek out the limelight. Rather, he is content with playing behind-the-scenes roles where action and organization are required. He likes to make things happen, but on a step-by-step basis.

Because he is not deeply introspective or self-analytical, he is sometimes naive or insensitive to the subtleties of feelings. At the same time, he is a very well-intentioned individual and conveys this to others through his sincerity and openness. He tends to have some difficulty with analyzing his own strengths and shortcomings and, for this reason, can sometimes fail to foresee his impact. Nevertheless, he listens to criticism and can benefit from the kind of criticism that is concretely put and well spelled out. He can be judgmental or intolerant of shortcomings, because he tends to measure others in his own terms. As he learns to reinterpret motives, his tolerance increases.

Socially, he is a rather sincere, unpretentious, modest, and pleasant person. Others would see him as very dependable, loyal, responsible, and dedicated, and very willing to pitch in to a group effort. He is quite caring toward others, and others would also see him as genuine. His relationships tend to be lasting and he maintains a high degree of interpersonal consistency. While he tends to keep his feelings to himself, his good intentions are evident. He is not highly diplomatic or subtle in his interactions, emphasizing a straightforward directness and frankness instead. He can assert himself and his leadership, particularly when he feels on safe ground and within his area of knowledge and expertise.

He is hard working, dedicated, persistent, determined, conscientious, and reliable. He is very company oriented. He enjoys, and is best at, concrete, practical, and structured activities involving systemizing, organizing, and implementing. He can experience difficulty when ambiguity is encountered unless a high degree of structure is provided. He responds best, then to fairly explicit direction and guidance on a continuing basis. The more concrete and specific his mandate and the more tied to finite results, the more effectively he can implement his part of an abstract goal and be left to his own devices.

His management style with subordinates is concerned, fair, compassionate, steady, and consistent. He is not a particularly subtle or sophisticated manager, but his genuineness comes through, and he does provide a model of dedication and loyalty. He is stronger in providing task leadership than conceptual leadership. He emphasizes strict controls and systems and can have some difficulty when more flexible approaches or systems are needed.

CONCLUSIONS AND PROGNOSIS

Mr. ———— is a stable and responsible person who functions best in systematizing and organizing activities of a tangible and factual nature. He is a loyal and hard-working employee with a good deal of dedication to the company, and is responsive to its expectations.

This evaluation was precipitated by mutual continuing concerns between Mr. ———— and his present manager regarding a lack of fit between his manager's expectations and Mr. ————'s performance. It is hypothesized that the frustrations each has encountered result, at least in part, from some of the differences in intellectual capacity and style between the two individuals. It seems likely, for example, that some of the more conceptually far-reaching expectations are beyond Mr. ————'s zone of competence and comfort. It would be helpful, then, to reshape the expectations to fit a more concrete implementation-oriented style. Providing him with greater continuing direction, structure, and clarity would also be helpful. Mr. ———— also benefits from expressions of appreciation for sincere effort.

It is suggested that the two sit down with the help of the psychologist and, in light of this evaluation, with a view toward taking better advantage of the particular abilities that Mr. ———— brings to the company.

Recent levels of frustration on both person's parts, as well as the pressure and overwork that Mr. ——— has imposed upon himself in his sincere attempt to meet the expectations as he has understood them, are not in anyone's best interests. A change in either job definition and responsibilities or supervisory style and expectations would clearly be helpful. He is the kind of person who can benefit from a concrete, "teaching" style on the part of his manager, one which focuses on specific methods, goals, and alternatives.

Mr. ———'s personal growth would be facilitated by his learning to relax a little more and to put himself under less internal pressure, learning to take a deep breath, to step back, and to look at sources of frustrations. He owes it to himself to do what is necessary in order to enjoy more and to be frustrated less, and especially to learn to recognize when enough is enough. Supportive reminders to this end from his manager might also help him lessen his inner intensity level.

In addition, he might want to look at ways of improving his sophistication with regard to the interpersonal side of management as well as establishing an intellectual framework for his managerial behavior. He might consider doing so by means of seminars or courses—especially very practical ones—in the interpersonal area of management in order better to assess his impact, increase his sensitivity, and refine his natural skills. Consistent with the points raised above is the need for him to be careful as his career progresses not to take on overly conceptual challenges. His strengths, rather, are more in concrete implementation, and it is felt that this is where he would best concentrate his talents. At this point in his career, it is suggested that he consider taking stock of himself and working harder at going with his strengths than at overcoming his weaknesses. In this way, he will be more likely to add to his solid record of achievement.

PSYCHOLOGICAL STUDY 4
Systems Manager, Age 34

Ms. ——— is in the upper 2 percent of the general population in her current level of general intellectual function-ing and problem-solving ability. She is, therefore, able to handle a wide range of problems at both an abstract and a concrete level. She is a relatively expansive thinker with a very strongly analytical mind and a capacity for comprehensiveness. She is analytically reflective, resourceful, alert, decisive, and incisive in her thinking. Logical and rational in style, she nevertheless appreciates shades of gray and can operate fluidly with intangibles as well as facts and figures. She emphasizes the tangible, however, and tends to make less use of her intuitions than she could. She is willing to take intellectual risks and can handle ambiguity, although she prefers putting a structure upon it. While not cautiously detailistic, narrow, or picayune, she does have a strong need to achieve intellectual closure, to feel she has control over her data, and this, sometimes, leads her to focus *inward* more and *outward* less.

A results-oriented thinker with a strongly practical and pragmatic side, she is very inquisitive, enjoys intellectual challenges, and tries to test her own limits and to stretch. She is often sound and level-headed in her judgments, looking for long-term implications and ramifications.

She is characterized by intellectual integrity and is basically open-minded and receptive. Yet there is a dogged, persistent quality to her thinking that sometimes leads to a kind of stubbornness despite her overall breadth and openness. She can force an issue into a framework or toward a conclusion; and it is the forced or relentless quality of her approach that can lead to some diminution of her ability to get outside herself in her own thinking, or outside of the facts at hand. She is a self-scrutinizing thinker who tries to filter and reflect but, on occasion, her inner intensity is so powerful as to obscure the dimmer shadows. She is, then, much stronger where the acuteness of a laser beam is the requirement than where the need is for night vision.

A late-maturing individual, she has recently grown a great deal, although, as she herself recognizes, she still has a way to go. She is very challenge-oriented and willing to test herself, to risk, and to change. She is self-demanding to a fault and very responsible, and she is characterized by integrity and a sense of values. There is an edge of intense self-demand, impatience, egocentrism, and relentlessness that, on occasion, leads her to push against barriers and obstacles rather than to flow with and around them. This intensity reflects an underlying wish to still prove herself.

Deep down, her self-concept remains somewhat underdeveloped, and there is a part of her that never feels content, that doubts her successes and her inherent legitimacy, that drives her to overcompensate. She tends to take herself for granted and to fail to grant herself acceptance, making her satisfactions transitory and leaving her with a feeling of being unquenched, of something still missing. As a result, she has too great a need to win, to press her will, and, as the tensions this creates build, her mood and temper can get the better of her. While often acutely aware of many of these characteristics and intensely desirous of sorting them out, she would have to learn to ease off, even on her own growth, in order to facilitate it. That is, it would help her to learn to *allow* rather than always to *forge* her progress.

She is a stable person who channels much of her intense energy and high self-demand into mature and constructive goal attainment. The same relentless energy that can lead her into difficulty is also her strength in that she seldom quits or withdraws before a problem is solved or an issue handled. Growth oriented and expansive in outlook, she is easily stimulated by the pursuit of possibilities. She is a highly proactive, self-initiating individual with a strong capacity for self-reliance and survival. Her resiliency is strong but is diminished by her intensity.

She very much wants to make an impact, to make things happen, to be in authority, to be at the controls. She is deeply motivated toward self-control and demonstrating her will power through determination, and persistence is important to her. She needs to feel that she is her own person, and she strives to achieve self-autonomy, independence, freedom of action, and freedom from restriction. She handles her independence effectively, although, to the degree that her self-concept is not fully developed, she lacks some of the stabilizing directionality that could foster her ultimate expression of independence. As a result, she can be at loose ends under stress or without support, and there is, then, a subtle dependence that underlies her fierce independence. She is a team player and likes cooperative environments and interdependent relationships. Thus, her independence does not lead her toward isolation or solitariness. She enjoys participating with and leading others.

She is a builder, a competitive and goal-oriented person who strives toward achievement and who likes to measure her success. Enduring and winning are, for her, ends in themselves. Prestige, status, or the admiration of others is less important than the inherent success. She dislikes details, routine, and stagnation, and she is a promoter of activity and change. She also has a strongly perfectionistic side that results in her need to make everything come out "right."

Her insights into herself and into other people are generally somewhat above average. She has a high degree of intellectual recognition of her own strengths and shortcomings, as well as those of others. Her intuitive grasp of the subtle ramifications and implications of these characteristics is less strong. That is, she has learned to be self-analytical, but she can have difficulty tuning in to the intuitive, both in herself and in others. This leads her to a kind of insensitivity and often reflects her churning intensity. This, in turn, can reduce her comfort, ease, and acuteness in addressing issues of emotion and insight.

She is receptive to criticism, does not externalize blame, and is a basically nondefensive, honest, open, sincere, deep, and self-accountable person, although she could pay better attention to her feelings. Her ability to benefit from criticism is facilitated by her growth orientation as well as her capacity to conceptualize.

Socially, she is forceful, dominant, aggressive, dynamic, unpretentious, and intense. She can lack diplomacy, tact, and subtlety, and is somewhat "rough around the edges" and occasionally overbearing. Nevertheless, she does tend to wear well owing to her dedication, energy, and the fact that her good intentions usually surface one way or the other. She does *care,* but it is sometimes difficult for her to allow or to express intimacy. She is willing to pitch in, and she is the kind of person others perceive as a genuine contributor. Under pressure, she is inclined to overcontrol and to dominate. She tends to see interpersonal barriers as a dichotomy between pushing or quitting, without fully considering eliciting, and has yet to find a fully satisfactory comfort zone in such situations.

She has a very strong sense of urgency and is a persistent and determined worker. Dedicated, reliable, responsible, and dependable, she is a "take charge" type of manager who maintains firm controls. She is less effective in eliciting followership, and she recognizes this and gives it more than just lip service. She can be impatient, overcontrolling, underdelegating, and too task oriented or pressuring.

She is inclined to adopt a good sense of business perspective and business direction. Action oriented and self-starting, she is a strong prime mover who is willing to make waves to achieve objectives. Her intelligence equips her well to handle the analytical and conceptual issues that come her way. She plans, looks ahead, maintains a business focus, maintains controls, and provides challenges to her subordinates that offer them the possibility of testing and stretching. She is concerned about developing subordinates, but can let it take second place, and she tends to have to "work at" being a manager. Her subordinates would see her as well meaning, fair, demanding, very goal oriented, and usually—but not always—respectful. She is most effective when her manager challenges her, but allows her freedom and latitude in meeting objectives. Ongoing feedback and discussion regarding her interpersonal style would also be beneficial, especially when she is dealing with interpersonal barriers.

CONCLUSIONS AND PROGNOSIS

Ms. ——— is an effective strategic business thinker and analyzer with a high intellectual capacity. She is a goal-oriented achiever with a strong sense of urgency, a willingness to create change, and a dedication to a sense of purpose. She is self-reliant and self-determined.

Were she able to mobilize the courage she employs in facing

the outer world in the service of accepting herself *as is,* she would go a long way toward quenching the inner thirst that drives her to be too relentless, too impatient, too driven, and too prone to having to prove. She would benefit from learning better to distinguish between introspective reflection and cross-examination of self. Growth here would help her to flow better with rather than against adversities and obstacles. True satisfactions can come from within. Unpressured consultations initiated as a result of the feedback of this study would be beneficial in this respect, as would looking back on the roots of her feelings of being "less legitimate."

It is suggested that she consider keeping an eye on her tendency to make everything a priority, to work on managing more by *in*direction and elicitation, and to do less forcing of reality and more facing of reality regarding people's talents and limitations. It is suggested that she also put more time and structure into focusing on developing her subordinates and relaxing as she does so in order to be better able to sense the more subtle vibrations. She might well want to consider attendance at seminars, workshops, or courses of an interpersonal/managerial/self-reflective nature, in order to assess her impact better, to learn more about the developmental process, and to think more about her own personal growth. Greater acceptance of herself, as well as others, will allow her to redirect her efforts in a manner that coordinates with the organizational ebb and flow. Her manager can facilitate the process by recognizing that Ms. ——— places more than enough pressure on herself to achieve, and by encouraging her to "take a deep breath," to limit her priorities realistically, and more patiently to adapt to the pace of others. There is no risk that she will become too low key. Her manager can also help by modeling the value of warm support and encouragement, perhaps demonstrating ways in which informality and relatively easy-going, non-pressure-packed discussions can be developmental and constructive.

Ms. ——— recognizes that she is at an important plateau in her career, and her desire to capitalize on that recognition is deeply earnest and deeply felt.

It is likely to be true that her further development as a

manager and developer of others will reflect her success in making the next steps she needs to make. These steps can be elusive, in that making them will take not the force but the courage to call forth her inner self and to allow her strength and her growing edge to be there for her.

PSYCHOLOGICAL STUDY 5
Engineering Director, Age 46

Mr. ———— falls in the top 5 percent of the general population in his current level of intellectual functioning and problem-solving ability. He is able to handle a wide range of issues comprehensively and conceptually. His intellectual style is careful, structured, methodical, and analytical. A level-headed thinker, he is focused on the relevant. He is inclined to emphasize the logical, rational, and objective components of a problem, and to look for practical and down-to-earth solutions. He digs deep and stresses preparedness and avoidance of risk, emphasizing the tangible and the finite over the intuitive, the creative, and the indefinite.

He is a person with a high level of intellectual integrity and good tolerance for ambiguity. He has a strong capacity for seeing and considering the points of view of others and for blending inputs into his own decisional framework.

Looking before he leaps, he is rather considered, deliberate, and reflective in his style of decision making. He is organized, thorough, precise, and probing, seldom merely skimming the surface. When he errs, it is on the side of caution, tradition, convention, and, occasionally, indecision. He is fairly easily stimulated by intellectual challenges. His curiosity helps him to broaden his intellectual range despite his cautiously analytical style. He is not particularly narrow, but he could be broader and more intellectually spontaneous.

He has a high level of personal integrity and a well-developed and well-integrated value system. He tends toward introversion and self-inhibition in an interpersonal or expressive context. Yet he is able to experience connectedness with his environment and with the other people in it. He is more of a giver than a taker. He is an emotionally well-centered and resilient individual.

He has a strong sense of responsibility, reciprocity, and obligation. At times, in fact, he can become overly responsible and stoic out of his sense of obligation. His basic nature is modest; however, over the years, he has developed confidence as well as a positive self-image and level of self-acceptance. While he is challenge oriented, he is, nevertheless, rather conservative and inclined to be more restrictive than expansive in his behavior and outlook. Thus, he seeks moderation and security, and he prefers to operate within boundaries and given parameters. He has the personal maturity to be constructive and to not become too narrow, but his inclinations are toward the predictable and the stable. Without external input, he can remain passive. He could, then, be more self-initiating and take more risks.

He is motivated by a sense of community obligation, but prestige, status, and recognition are not of particular importance to him. More humble than prideful, he is inclined to play behind-the-scenes roles, to let others take the credit, and to avoid the spotlight. He likes to operate in a facilitative, participative, and partnerly atmosphere, where there is a high degree of consensus, mutual facilitation, and teamwork. He is inclined to harmonize and to blend in rather than to stand out or strike out on his own. He tends to overconform.

His overall drive and energy are above average. He is responsive to stimulation and opportunities and presses toward his goals with self-discipline and persistence. He prefers environments, however, that are predictable, stable, and consistent. He is not deeply competitive or financially ambitious. It is important to him to be able to put order in his world, and he uses problem-solving and intellectual control as a means of doing so.

His insights into himself and into other people are generally above average. He has developed depth in his insights and a sense of perspective toward himself as well as others. While not deeply introspective, he is receptive to criticism and open to self-reflection, and he knows how to gain from it. He is a good listener. Although inclined to stress logic over emotion and intuition, he has learned to balance and adapt his more straightforward and logical style to the needs of others. He is, therefore, capable of changing his behavior according to the situation.

Others see him as honest, trusting, reliable, dependable, sincere, and unpretentious. His leadership is low key, but he makes his presence felt. More inclined toward facilitation than confrontation or dynamic persuasiveness, he has learned to use his style with staying power. He is a cooperative contributor, willing to pitch in, and a receptive team player. He is steady, calm, easygoing, and relatively reserved. He maintains some distance between himself and others regarding emotional intimacy. As a result others may take awhile to warm up to him, and some people see him as cool or detached, particularly initially. Subordinates would view him as fair, considerate, steady, predictable, and concerned about their development, but somewhat less involved than some would prefer.

His managerial style is participative, and he has learned to work through others, to delegate autonomy, and to lead by example. He is a harmonizing and stabilizing force with a very responsible, dependable, and hard-working approach, consciously representing the values of the organization. He is rather organized and, by nature, tends to rely on controls and systems. He has worked on loosening the reins, but he could probably loosen them some more. Consistent with his generally conservative posture, his style is more conducive to evolution than to dynamic change or bold innovation. He responds well to a sense of partnership and mutuality with his boss, and, in fact, needs it; he benefits from external stimulation. He can be proactive in a steady and consistent manner, but he is at his best when his energies are catalyzed.

CONCLUSIONS AND PROGNOSIS

Mr. ———'s characteristics fit with being a solid contributor and a strong team player. A mature individual of high intellectual capacity, he can contribute technically, but has learned to stress facilitating the involvement of others over emphasizing his own engineering expertise. He wears well interpersonally, but he could be less reserved and confront people more directly. He is developmentally oriented and has many of the intellectual and perceptive elements that go into understanding others.

At one level, he could round out his understanding with workshops, seminars, or courses in the interpersonal area, particularly those that provide a well-ordered framework for managing others. At a deeper level, in order to maximize his contributions, it will be important for him to look at the degree to which his aversion to risk can inhibit his ability to be proactive and self-initiating, with a goal of achieving greater impact on the organization. In this regard, it is suggested that he consider seeking intellectual stimulation and "stretching" via readings, seminars, and courses that provoke him to think beyond the conventional and the status quo.

Thus, Mr. ——— and his organization are likely to find it quite satisfactory to focus on continuing the development of his clear strengths—for example, his team building. The greater challenge is for him to develop a greater number of style options. He and his manager, for example, might look for small steps Mr. ——— could take in asserting a more direct or constructively confrontational style. Mr. ——— is likely to experience the greatest growth with a small step-at-a-time approach to his own development. His further growth is likely to be moderate and steady.

References

Allport, G. W. (1931). What is a trait of personality? *Journal of Abnormal and Social Psychology, 25,* 368–372.

Allport, G. W. (1955). *Becoming.* New Haven, CT: Yale University Press.

Allport, G. W. (1960). The open system in personality theory. *Journal of Abnormal and Social Psychology, 61,* 301–309.

Anastasi, A. (1982). *Psychological testing.* (5th ed.). New York: Macmillan.

Anderson, A. R. & Moore, O. K. (1959). *Autoelic folk models.* New Haven, CT: ONR Technical Report.

Argyris, C. (1985). *Strategy change and defensive routines.* Boston: Pitman Publishing.

Asante, M. K., Newmark, E., & Blake, C. A. (Eds.). (1980). *Handbook of intercultural communication.* Beverly Hills, CA: Sage.

Atkinson, J. W. (Ed.). (1958). *Motives in fantasy, action, and society.* Princeton, NJ: Van Nostrand Reinhold.

Bakal, D. A. (1979). *Psychology and medicine: psychobiological dimensions of health and illness.* New York: Springer.

Baltes, P. B. & Brim, O. G. (Eds.). (1981). *Life-span development and behavior* (Vol. 3). New York: Academic Press.

Baltes, P. B. & Schaie, K. W. (Eds.). (1973). *Life-span development psychology: Personality and socialization.* New York: Academic Press.

Bandura, A. (1969). *Principles of behavior modification.* New York: Holt, Rinehart & Winston.

Bandura, A. (1986). *Social foundations of thought and action: A social cognitive theory.* Englewood Cliffs, NJ: Prentice-Hall.

Barber, J. & Adrian, C. (Eds.). (1988). *Psychological approaches to the management of pain.* New York: Brunner/Mazel.

Barber, T. X. (1982). Hypnosuggestive procedures in the treatment of clinical pain. In T. Millon, C. Green, & R. Meagher (Eds.), *Handbook of clinical health psychology.* New York: Plenum Press.

Barker, P. A. (1985). *Using metaphors in psychotherapy.* New York: Brunner/ Mazel.

167

168   PSYCHOLOGICAL CONSULTING TO MANAGEMENT

Bass, B. M. (1965). *Organizational psychology.* Boston: Allyn & Bacon.

Baum, A. & Singer, J. (Eds.). (1983). *Handbook of psychology and health.* Hillsdale, NJ: Erlbaum.

Bazerman, M. H. (1986). *Human judgment in managerial decision making.* New York: John Wiley.

Beck, A. T. (1976). *Cognitive therapy and emotional disorders.* New York: International Universities Press.

Beckhard, R. & Harris, R. T. (1987). *Organizational transitions: Managing complex change* (2nd ed.). Reading, MA: Addison-Wesley.

Beier, E. G. (1988, March). Toward a unified theory of psychotherapy: Some basic assumptions. *Clinician's Research Digest.* Supplemental Bulletin.

Bellows, R. (1961). *Psychology of personnel in business and industry* (3rd ed.). Englewood Cliffs, NJ: Prentice-Hall.

Bennis, W., Benne, K. D., Chin, R. & Corey, K. E. (1975). *The planning of change* (3rd ed.). New York: Holt, Rinehart & Winston.

Bennis, W. & Nanus, B. (1985) *Leaders: The strategies for taking charge.* New York: Harper & Row.

Berger, J., Cohen, B. P., & Zelditch, M., Jr. (1966). Status characteristics and expectation states. In Berger, J., Cohen, B. P., Zelditch, M., Jr., & Anderson, B. (Eds.), *Sociological theories in progress.* Boston: Houghton-Mifflin.

Beutler, L. E. (1983). *Electic psychotherapy: a systematic approach.* New York: Pergamon Press.

Billow, R. (1977). Metaphor: A review of the psychological literature. *Psychological Bulletin, 84,* 81–92.

Blake, R. R. & Mouton, J. S. (1969). *Building a dynamic corporation through grid organization development.* Reading, MA: Addison-Wesley.

Bond, L. & Rosen, J. (1980). *Competence and coping during adulthood.* Hanover, NH: University Press of New England.

Bonica, J. J. (Ed.). (1980). *Pain.* New York: Raven Press.

Bradley, L. A. & Prokop, C. K. (Eds.). (1980). *Medical psychology: Contributions to behavioral medicine.* New York: Academic Press.

Bray, D. M., Campbell, K. J., & Grant, D. L. (1974). *Formative years in business: A long-term AT&T study of managerial lives.* New York: John Wiley.

Bridges, W. E. (1980). *Transitions: Making sense of life's changes.* Reading, MA: Addison-Wesley.

Brim, O. G., Jr. (1976). Theories of male mid-life crisis. *The Counseling Psychologist, 6,* 2–9.

Bronowski, J. (1973). *The ascent of man.* Boston: Little, Brown.

Brown, D. & Brooks, L., and Associates (1987). *Career choice and development.* San Francisco: Jossey-Bass.

Bryne, D. (1971). *The attraction paradigm.* New York: Academic Press.

Buckley, W. (1967). *Sociology and modern systems theory.* Englewood Cliffs, NJ: Prentice-Hall.

Buckley, W. (1968). *Modern systems research for the behavioral scientist.* Chicago: Aldine.

Bugental, J. F. T. (1987). *The art of the psychotherapist.* New York: Norton.

Burke, W. W. (1978). *The cutting edge: Current practice and theory in organization development.* San Diego: University Associates.

Burke, W. W. (1987). *Organization development: A normative view.* Reading, MA: Addison-Wesley.

Burrows, G. D., Collison, D. R., & Dennerstein, L. (Eds.). (1979). *Hypnosis 1979.* New York: Elsevier/North Holland.

Campbell, J. P., Campbell, R. J., & Associates (1988). *Productivity in organizations.* San Francisco: Jossey-Bass.

Campbell, J. P., Dunnette, M. D., Lawler, E. E., & Weick, K. E., Jr. (1970). *Managerial behavior, performance, and effectiveness.* New York: McGraw-Hill.

Carsman, M. J. (1983). Individual career planning and counseling. In J. S. J. Manuso (Ed.), *Occupational clinical psychology.* New York: Praeger.

Cheek, D. B. & LeCron, L. M. (1968). *Clinical hypnotherapy.* New York: Grune & Stratton.

Chesney, M. A. & Feuerstein, M. (1979). Behavioral medicine in the occupational setting. In J. McNamara (Ed.), *Behavioral medicine.* Kalamazoo, MI: Behaviordelia.

Clark, H. H. & Clark, E. V. (1977). *Psychology and language.* New York: Harcourt Brace Jovanovich.

Clionsky, M. I. (1983). Assertiveness training for corporate executives. In J. S. J. Manuso (Ed.), *Occupational clinical psychology.* New York: Praeger.

Cofer, C. N. & Appley, M. H. (1964). *Motivation: Therapy and research.* New York: John Wiley.

Cole, M. & Scribner, S. (1974). *Culture and thought.* New York: John Wiley.

Connor, R. A. & Davidson, J. P. (1985). *Marketing your consulting and professional services.* New York: John Wiley.

Cooper, C. L. & Payne, R. L. (Eds.). (1988). *Causes, coping, and consequences of stress at work.* New York: John Wiley.

Cooper, C. L. & Robertson, I. T. (Eds.). (1988). *International review of industrial and organizational psychology.* New York: John Wiley.

Crasilneck, H. B. & Hall, J. A. (1975). *Clinical hypnosis: Principles and applications.* New York: Grune & Stratton.

Dagenais, J. G. (1972). *Models of man.* The Hague: Nijhoff.

Daniel, N. (1975). *The cultural barrier: Problems in the exchange of ideas.* Edinburgh: University Press.

Datan, N. & Ginsberg, L. (1976). *Life-span development psychology: Normative life crises.* New York: Academic Press.

Deci, E. L. (1972). The effects of contingent and non-contingent rewards and controls on intrinsic motivation. *Organization Behavior and Human Performance, 8,* 217–229.

DuBrin, Andrew J. (1972). *The practice of managerial psychology.* Elmsford, NY: Pergamon Press.

Dunnette, M. D. (Ed.). (1976). *Handbook of industrial and organizational psychology.* Skokie, IL: Rand McNally.

Dyer, L. (Ed.). (1976). *Careers in organizations: Individual planning and organizational development.* Ithaca, NY: New York State School of Industrial and Labor Relations Cornell University.

Dyer, W. G. (1987). *Team building: Issues and alternatives* (2nd ed.). Reading, MA: Addison-Wesley.

Ellis, A. (1962). *Reason and emotion in psychotherapy.* New York: Lyle Stuart.

Ellis, A. (1971). *Growth through reason: Verbatim cases in rational-emotive therapy.* Palo Alto, CA: Science and Behavior Books.

Engdahl, R. H., Walsh, D. C., & Goldbeck, W. (Eds.). (1980). *Mental wellness programs for employees.* New York: Springer-Verlag.

Epstein, S. (1980). The self-concept: A review and the proposal of an integrated theory of personality. In E. Staub (Ed.), *Personality: Basic issues and current research.* Englewood Cliffs, NJ: Prentice-Hall.

Erickson, M. H., Rossi, E. L., & Rossi, S. I. (1976). *Hypnotic realities: The induction of clinical hypnosis and forms of indirect suggestion.* New York: Irvington.

Erickson, M. H. & Rossi, E. L. (1979). *Hypnotherapy: An exploratory casebook.* New York: Irvington.

Erikson, E. H. (1950). *Childhood and society.* New York: Norton.

Erikson, E. H. (1959). Identity and the life cycle. *Psychological Issues, 1,* 1.

Erikson, E. H. (1980). *Identity and the life cycle.* New York: Norton.

Evans, M. B. (1988). The role of metaphor in psychotherapy and personality change: A theoretical reformulation. *Psychotherapy, 25,* 4, 543–551.

Eyde, L. D. & Kowal, D. M. (1987). Computerized test interpretation services: Ethical and professional concerns regarding U.S. producers and users. *Applied Psychology: An International Review, 36,* (3–4), 401–417.

Fear, R. A. (1980). *The evaluation interview.* New York: McGraw-Hill.

Figler, H. R. (1978). *Overcoming executive mid-life crisis.* New York: McGraw-Hill.

Fiske, S. & Taylor, S. (1984). *Social cognition.* New York: Random House.

Flory, C. D. (Ed.). (1965). *Managers for tomorrow.* New York: New American Library.

Follmann, J. F., Jr. (1978). *Helping the troubled employee.* New York: AMACOM.

Fowler, R. D. & Butcher, J. N. (1987). International applications of computer-based testing and interpretation. *Applied Psychology: An International Review, 36,* (3–4), 419–429.

Frank, J. D. (1981). Therapeutic components shared by all psychotherapies. In J. H. Harvey & M. M. Parks (Eds.), *The master lecture series, vol. 1. Psychotherapy research and behavior change.* Washington, DC: American Psychological Association.

French, J. R. P., Caplan, R., & Van Harrison, R. (Eds.). (1982). *The mechanisms of job stress and strain.* New York: John Wiley.

French, W. L. & Bell, C. H. (1973). *Organization development.* Englewood Cliffs, NJ: Prentice-Hall.

Galtung, J. (1980). *The true worlds.* New York: Free Press/Macmillan.

Galtung, J. (1981). *Social science information, 20* (6), 817–856.

Garfield, S. L. (1980). *Psychotherapy. An eclectic approach.* New York: John Wiley.

Gatchel, R. J. & Baum, A. (1983). *An introduction to health psychology.* Reading, MA: Addison-Wesley.

Gatchel, R. J., & Baum, A. (Eds.). (1982). *Behavioral medicine and clinical psychology: Overlapping areas.* Hillsdale, NJ: Erlbaum.

Gellerman, S. W. (1963). *Motivation and productivity.* New York: American Management Association.

Genst, M. & Genst, S. (1987). *Psychology and health.* Champaign, IL: Research Press.

Ghiselli, E. E. (1973). The validity of aptitude tests in personnel selection. *Personnel Psychology, 26,* 461–477.

Gibb, J. R. (1978). *Trust: a new view of personal and organizational development.* Los Angeles: The Guild of Tutors Press.

Gibson, E. J. (1969). *Principles of perceptual learning and development.* New York: Appleton-Century-Crofts.

Ginges, N. G. & Maynard, W. S. (1983). Intercultural aspects of organizational effectiveness. In Landis, E. & Brislin, R. W. (Eds.), *Handbook of intercultural training* (Vol. II, Issues in Training Methodology). New York: Pergamon Press.

Glanzer, M. (1958). Curiosity, exploratory drive, and stimulus satiation. *Psychological Bulletin, 55,* 302–315.

Glaser, E. M. (1958). Psychological consulting with executives: A clinical approach. *American Psychologist, 13,* 8, 1–8.

Goldberg, P. (1978). *Executive health.* New York: McGraw-Hill.

Goldfried, M. R. (Ed.). (1982). *Converging themes in psychotherapy.* New York: Springer.

Goldfried, M. R. & Davison, G. C. (1976). *Clinical behavior therapy.* New York: Holt, Rinehart & Winston.

Goldman, L. (1971). *Using tests in counseling* (2nd ed.). Santa Monica, CA: Goodyear.

Goleman, D. (1985). *Vital lies, simple truths: The psychology of self-deception.* New York: Simon & Schuster.

Gordon, D. (1978). *Therapeutic metaphors.* Cupertino, CA: Meta Publications.

Gould, M. I. (1970). Counseling for self-development. *Personnel Journal, 49,* 3, 226–234.

Gould R. L. (1978). *Transformations: Growth & change in adult life.* New York: Simon & Schuster.

Grant, D. L. (1980). Issues in personnel selection. *Professional Psychology, 11,* 3, 369–384.

Grant, D. L., Katkovsky, W., & Bray, D. W., (1967). Contributions of project techniques to assessment of management potential. *Journal of Applied Psychology, 51,* 226–232.

Greenwald, A. G. (1980). The totalitarian ego: Fabrication and revision of personal history. *American Psychologist, 35,* 603–613.

Gubrium, J. F. & Buckholdt, D. R. (1977). *Toward maturity: The social processing of human development.* San Francisco: Jossey-Bass.

Gutteridge, T. G. (Ed.). (1980). *Career planning and development: Perspectives of the individual and the organization.* Madison, WI: American Society for Training and Development.

Guzzo, R. A. (1979). Types of rewards, cognitions, and work motivation. *Academy of Management Review, 4,* 75–86.

Hackman, J. R. & Oldham, G. (1980). *Work redesign.* Reading, MA: Addison Wesley.

Haire, M. (1959). Psychological problems relevant to business and industry. *Psychological Bulletin, 56,* 169–194.

Haley, J. (1984). *Ordeal Therapy.* San Francisco: Jossey-Bass.

Hall, D. T. (1976). *Careers in organizations.* Pacific Palisades, CA: Goodyear.

Hall, D. T., Bowen, D. D., Lewicki, R. J., & Hall, F. S. (1982). *Experiences in management and organizational behavior.* New York: John Wiley.

Hamberger, J. K. & Lohr, J. M. (1988). *Stress and stress management.* New York: Springer.

Hampden-Turner, C. (1981). *Maps of the mind.* New York: Macmillan.

Hartman, B. J. (1980). *A system of hypnotherapy.* Chicago: Nelson-Hall.

Hartmann, H. (1958). *Ego psychology and the problem of adaptation.* (D. Rapaport, Trans.) New York: International Universities Press. (Originally published in German in 1939.)

Hendrick, I. (1942). Instinct and the ego during infancy. *Psychoanalytic Quarterly, 11,* 35–58.

Herd, J. A. & Fox, B. H. (Eds.). (1981). *Perspectives on behavioral medicine.* New York: Academic Press.

Herr, E. L. & Cramer, S. H. (1979). *Career guidance through the life span.* Boston: Little, Brown.

Hertzberg, F., Mausner, B., & Synderman, B. (1959). *The motivation to work* (2nd ed.). New York: John Wiley.

Hilgard, E. R. & Hilgard, J. R. (1975). *Hypnosis in the relief of pain.* Los Altos, CA: Kaufmann.

Hogan, R. & Nicholson, R. A. (1988). The meaning of personality test scores. *American Psychologist, 43,* 8, 621–626.

Holland, J. L. (1985). *Making vocational choices: A theory of careers.* Englewood Cliffs, NJ: Prentice-Hall.

Holland, J. L., Magoon, T., & Spokane, A. R. (1981). Counseling psychology: Career intervention and related research and theory. *Annual review of psychology, 32,* 279–305.

Huba, G. J. (1987). On probabilistic computer-based test interpretations and other expert systems. *Applied Psychology: An International Review, 36,* 357–373.

Jahoda, M. (1953). The meaning of psychological health. *Social Casework, 34,* 349–354.

Jay, A. (1968). *Management & Machiavelli: An inquiry into the politics of corporate life.* New York: Holt, Rinehart & Winston.

Jennings, E. E. (1967). *Executive success: Stresses, problems, and adjustments.* New York: Appleton-Century-Crofts.

Kagan, J. (1987). The meanings of personality predicates. *American Psychologist, 43,* 8, 614–620.

Kahn, R. L. (1980). *Work and health.* New York: John Wiley.

Kahn, R. L., Wolfe, D. M., Quinn, R. P., & Snoek, R. A. (1964). *Organizational stress: Studies in role conflict and ambiguity.* New York: John Wiley.

Kanter, R. M. (1977a). *Men and women of the corporation.* New York: Basic Books.

Kanter, R. M. (1977b). *Work and family in the United States: A critical review and agenda for research and policy.* New York: Russell Sage Foundation.

Katz, D. & Kahn, R. (1966). *The social psychology of organization.* New York: John Wiley.

Kelley, G. A. (1970). A brief introduction to personal construct theory. In D. Bannister (Ed.), *Perspectives in personal construct theory.* New York: Academic Press.

Kenrick & Funder (1988). Profiting from controversy: Lessons from the person–situation debate. *American Psychologist, 43,* (1), 23–34.

Kiefhaber, A. & Goldbeck, W. B. (1979). *Employee mental wellness programs: A WBGH survey.* Washington, DC: Washington Business Group on Health.

Klegon, D. (1978). The sociology of professions: An emerging perspective. *Sociology of work and occupations, 5,* 259–283.

Kluckhohn, F. & Strodbeck, F. (1961). *Variations in value orientations.* New York: Harper & Row.

Kohn, M. & Schooler, C. (1983). *Work and personality: An inquiry into the impact of social stratification.* Norwood, NJ: Ablex.

Kornhauser, A. (1965). *Mental health of the industrial worker: A Detroit study.* New York: John Wiley.

Kotler, P. & Bloom, P. (1984). *Marketing professional services.* Englewood Cliffs, NJ: Prentice Hall.

Kotter, J. P., Faux, V. A., & McArthur, C. C. (1978). *Self assessment and career development.* Englewood Cliffs, NJ: Prentice-Hall.

Krasner, L. & Ullmann, L. P. (1973). *Behavior influence and personality: The social matrix of human action.* New York: Holt, Rinehart & Winston.

Krumboltz, J. D., & Hamel, D. A. (Eds.). (1982). *Assessing career development.* Palo Alto, CA: Mayfield.

Langer, J. (1969). *Theories of development.* New York: Holt, Rinehart & Winston.

Lawler, E. E. (1966). Manager's attitudes towards how their pay is and should be determined. *Journal of Applied Psychology, 50,* 273–279.

Lawler, E. E. (1971). *Pay and organizational effectiveness: A psychological view.* New York: McGraw-Hill.

Lawler, E. E. (1981). *Pay and organization development.* Reading, MA: Addison-Wesley.

Lawrence, P. R. & Lorsch, J. W. (1969). *Developing organizations: Diagnosis and action.* Reading, MA: Addison-Wesley.

Lazarus, R. S. & Folkman, S. (1984). *Stress, appraisal, and coping.* New York: Springer.

Leavy, S. A. & Freedman, L. Z. (1956). Psychoneurosis and economic life. *Social Problems, 4,* 55–67.

Levinson, D. (1978). *The seasons of a man's life.* New York: Knopf.

Levinson, H. (1964). *Emotional health: In the world of work.* New York: Harper & Row.

Levinson, H. (1970). *Executive stress.* New York: Harper & Row.

Levinson, H. (1972). Organizational diagnosis. Cambridge, MA: Harvard University Press.

Levinson, H. & Menninger, W. C. (1954). The machine that made pop. *Menninger Quarterly, 8,* (2): 20–26.

Levinson, H., Price, C. R., Munden, K. J., Mandl, H. J., & Soley, C. M. (1962). *Men, management and mental health.* Cambridge, MA: Harvard University Press.

Lezak, M. D., (1982). *Neuropsychological assessment.* New York: Oxford University Press.

Likert, R. (1961). *New patterns of management.* New York: McGraw-Hill.

Lippitt, R., Watson, J., & Westley, B. (1958). *Dynamics of planned change.* New York: Harcourt, Brace & World.

Lloyd, B. B. (1972). *Perception and cognition: A cross cultural perspective.* Baltimore: Penguin Books.

Lowenthal, M. F., Thurnher, M., & Chiriboga, D. (1976). *Four stages of life.* San Francisco: Jossey-Bass.

Magnusson, D. & Endler, N. S. (Eds.). (1977). *Personality at the cross-roads: Current issues in interactional psychology.* Hillsdale, NJ: Erlbaum.

Mahoney, M. J. (1974). *Cognition and behavior modification.* Cambridge, MA: Ballinger.

Mangham, I. M. (1978). *Interactions and interventions in organizations.* New York: John Wiley.

Manuso, J. S. J. (Ed.). (1983). *Occupational clinical psychology.* New York: Praeger.

Margulies, N. & Raia, A. P. (1972). *Organization development: Values, process and technology.* New York: McGraw-Hill.

Maslow, A. H. (1954). *Motivation and personality.* New York: Harper & Brothers.

Maslow, A. H. (1970). *Motivation and personality* (rev. ed.). New York: Harper & Brothers.

Maslow, A. H. (1971). *The farther reaches of human nature.* New York: Viking Press.

Matarazzo, J. D. (1980). Behavioral health and behavioral medicine: Frontiers for a new health psychology. *American psychologist, 35,* (9) 828–840.

McClelland, D. C., Atkinson, J. W., Clark, R. A., & Lowell, E. L. (1953). *The achievement motive.* New York: Appleton-Century-Crofts.

McCormick, E. J. & Ilgen, D. R. (1980). *Industrial psychology* (7th ed.). Englewood Cliffs, NJ: Prentice-Hall.

McLean, A. A. (1974). Mental health programs in industry. In S. Arieti (Ed.), *American handbook of psychiatry* (Vol. 2). New York: Basic Books.

McLean, A. A. (1979). *How to reduce occupational stress.* Lexington, MA: Addison-Wesley.

McLean, A. A. (Ed.). (1974). *Occupational stress.* Springfield, IL: Charles C. Thomas.

McLean, A. A. & Taylor, G. C. (1958). *Mental health in industry.* New York: McGraw-Hill.

McMurray, R. N. (1959). Mental illness in industry. *Harvard Business Review, 37,* 79–86.

McReynolds, P. (1975). *Advances in psychological assessment.* San Francisco: Jossey-Bass.

Meehl, P. E. (1978). Theoretical risks and tabular asterisks: Sir Karl, Sir Ronald, and the slow progress of soft psychology. *Journal of Consulting and Clinical Psychology, 46,* 806–834.

Meichenbaum, D. H. (1977). *Cognitive-behavior modification.* New York: Plenum.

Melamed, B. G. & Siegel, L. J. (1988). *Behavioral medicine.* New York: Springer.

Menninger, W. C. & Levinson, H. (1954). Industrial mental health: Observations and perspectives. *Menninger Quarterly 8* (3) : 1–13.

Miles, R. E. (1975). *Theories of management: Implications for organizational behaviour and development.* New York: McGraw-Hill.

Miller, M. M. (1979). *Therapeutic hypnosis.* New York: Human Services Press.

Millon, T. (1988). Personologic psychotherapy: Ten commandments for a posteclectic approach to integrative treatment. *Psychotherapy 25,* (2), 209–219.

Millon, T., Green, C., & Meagher, R. (Eds.). (1982). *Handbook of clinical health psychology.* New York: Plenum Press.

Miner, J. B. (1969). *Personnel psychology.* New York: Macmillan.

Mischel, W. (1968). *Personality and assessment.* New York: John Wiley.

Montross, D. H. & Shinkman, C. J. (Eds.). (1981). *Career development in the 1980s: Theory and practice.* Springfield, IL: Charles C. Thomas.

Moreland, K. L. (1987). Computer-based test interpretations: Advice to the consumer. *Applied Psychology: An International Review, 36* (3–4), 385–399.

Morgan, H. H. & Cogger, J. C. (1980). *The interviewer's manual.* New York: Drake Beam Morin.

Morgan, M. A. (1980). *Managing career development.* New York: Van Nostrand Reinhold.

Most, R. B. (1987). Levels of errors in computerized psychological inventories. *Applied Psychology: An International Review,* Vol. 36 (3–4), 375–383.

Most, R. B. & Glazer, H. I. (1983). Contemporary psychological assessment in organizational settings. In J. S. J. Manuso, *Occupational Clinical Psychology.* New York: Praeger.

Muench, G. A. (1960). A clinical psychologist's treatment of labor-management conflicts. *Personnel Psychology, 13,* 165–172.

Murphy, G. (1958). *Human potentialities.* New York: Basic Books.

Murray, H. A. (1938). *Exploration in personality.* New York: Oxford University Press.

Murray, H. A. (1951). Toward classification of interaction. In T. Parsons & E. A. Shils (Eds.), *Toward a general theory of action.* Cambridge, MA: Harvard University Press.

Murray, H. A. (1959). Preparations for the scaffold of a comprehensive system. In S. Koch (Ed.), *Psychology: A study of a science* (Vol. III). New York: McGraw-Hill.

Nadler, D. A. (1977). *Feedback and organization development.* Reading, MA: Addison-Wesley.

Neisser, V. (1976). *Cognition and reality: Principles and implications of cognitive psychology.* San Francisco: Freeman.

Nevis, E. C. (1987). *Organization consulting: A Gestalt approach.* New York: Gardner Press.

Nisbett, R. E. & Ross, L. (1980). *Human Inference: Strategies and shortcomings of social judgment.* Englewood Cliffs, NJ: Prentice-Hall.

Noland, R. L. (Ed.). (1973). *Industrial mental health and employee counseling.* New York: Behavioral Publications.

Norcross, J. C. (Ed.). (1986). *Handbook of Eclectic Psychotherapy.* New York: Brunner/Mazel.

Norman, W. H. & Scaramella, T. J. (1980). *Mid-Life: Development and clinical issues.* New York: Brunner/Mazel.

Novaco, R. (1975). *Anger control: The development and evaluation of an experimental treatment.* Lexington, MA: D. C. Heath.

Offer, D. & Sabshin, M. (Eds.). (1984). *Normality and the life cycle.* New York: Basic Books.

Offer, D. & Sabshin, M. (Eds.). (1988). *Normality: Context and Theory.* New York: Basic Books.

Ohmann, O. A. (1957). Executive Appraisal and Counseling. *Michigan Business Review, 9,* 18–25.

Omer, H. & London, P. (1988). Metamorphosis in psychotherapy: End of the systems era. *Psychotherapy, 25* (2), 171–179.

Osipow, S. H. (1983). *Theories of career development* (3rd ed.). Englewood Cliffs, NJ: Prentice-Hall.

Osipow, S. H., Doty, R., & Spokane, A. R. (1985). Occupational stress, strain, and coping across the lifespan. *Journal of Vocational Behavior, 27,* 98–108.

Philips, C. H. (1988). *The psychological management of chronic pain.* New York: Springer.

Pomerleau, O. F. & Brady, J. P. (Eds.). (1979). *Behavioral medicine: Theory and practice.* Baltimore: Williams & Wilkins.

Prediger, D. J. (1974). The role of assessment in career guidance. In E. Herr (Ed.), *Vocational guidance and human development.* Boston: Houghton Mifflin.

Price-Williams, D. R. (1975). *Explorations in cross-cultural psychology.* Los Angeles: Chandler & Sharp.

Pruyser, P. W. (1979). *The psychological examination.* New York: International Universities Press, Inc.

Rachman, S. (Ed.). (1980). *Medical psychology.* New York: Pergamon Press.

Raelin, J. A. (1986). *The clash of cultures: Managers and professionals.* Cambridge, MA: Harvard Business School Press.

Rogers, C. R. (1961). *On becoming a person.* Boston: Houghton Mifflin.

Rogers, C. R. (1969). Personal thoughts on teaching and learning. In C. R.

Rogers, *Freedom to learn: A view of what education might be*. Columbus, OH: Merrill.

Rogers, E. & Agarwala-Rogers, R. (1976). *Communication in organizations*. New York: Free Press.

Rosen, S. (Ed.). (1982). *My voice will go with you: The teaching tales of Milton H. Erickson, M.D.* New York: Norton.

Ross, L. (1977). The intuitive psychologist and his shortcomings: Distortions in the attribution process. In L. Berkowitz (Ed.), *Advances in experimental social psychology* (Vol. 10, pp. 174–221). New York: Academic Press.

Sadler, L. E. (1960). The counseling psychologist in business and industry. *Vocational Guidance Quarterly, 8,* 123–125.

Samovar, L. & Porter, R. (Eds.). (1985). *Intercultural communication: A reader* (4th ed.). Belmont, CA: Wadsworth.

Schein, E. H. (1965). *Organizational psychology*. Englewood Cliffs, NJ: Prentice–Hall.

Schein, E. H. (1969). *Process consultation: Its role in organizational development*. Reading, MA: Addison-Wesley.

Schein, E. H. (1973). *Professional education*. New York: McGraw-Hill.

Schein, E. H. (1978). *Career dynamics: Matching individual and organizational needs*. Reading, MA: Addison-Wesley.

Schein, E. H. (1985). *Career anchors: Discovering your real values*. San Diego: University Associates.

Schein, E. H. (1987). *Process consultation: Lessons for managers and consultants*. Reading, MA: Addison-Wesley.

Schilder, P. (1942). *Goals and desires of man: A psychological survey of life*. New York: Columbia University Press.

Schlenker, B. R. (Ed.). (1985). *The self and social life*. New York: McGraw-Hill.

Schmitz, H. V. (1981). *Executive and employee counseling: A handbook*. New York: The New York Business Group on Health.

Schmitz, H. V. (1983). Executive and employee counseling program models and their uses. In J. S. J. Manuso (Ed.), *Occupational clinical psychology*. New York: Praeger.

Schneider, D. (1973). Implicit personality theory: A review. *Psychological Bulletin, 79,* 294–309.

Schon, D. A. (1987). *Educating the reflective practitioner*. San Francisco: Jossey-Bass.

Schwab, D. P. & Dyer, L. (1973). The motivational impact of a compensation system on employee performance. *Organizational behavior and human performance, 9,* 215–225.

Schwartz, G. E. (1983). Stress management in occupational settings. In J. S. J. Manuso (Ed.), *Occupational clinical psychology*. New York: Praeger.

Selye, H. (1976). *The stress of life*. New York: McGraw-Hill.

Shaver, P. (Ed.). (1984). *Review of personality and social psychology: Emotions, relationships, and health*. Beverly Hills, CA: Sage.

Slosar, D. M. (1982). Utilizing the language of the unconsciousness. In Zeig, J. K. (Ed.), *Ericksonian approaches to hypnosis and psychotherapy*. New York: Brunner/Mazel.

Smelser, J. & Erikson, E. H. (Eds.). (1980). *Themes of work and love in adulthood.* Cambridge, MA: Harvard University Press.

Snyder, C. R. & Ford, C. E. (Eds.). (1987). *Coping with negative life events: Clinical and social psychological perspectives.* New York: Plenum Press.

Snyder, C. R. & Smith, T. W. (1982). Symptoms as self-handicapping strategies: The virtues of old wine in a new bottle. In G. Weary & H. Mirels (Eds.), *Integrations of clinical and social psychology* (pp. 104–127). New York: Oxford University Press.

Snyder, M. & Ickes, W. (1985). Personality and social behavior. In G. Lindzey & E. Aronson (Eds.), *Handbook of social psychology* (3rd ed., Vol. 2). Reading, MA: Addison-Wesley.

Souerwine, A. H. (1978). *Career strategies: Planning for personal achievement.* New York: AMACOM.

Spence, J. T. (1983). *Achievement and achievement motives: Psychological and sociological approaches.* San Francisco: W. H. Freeman.

Spiegel, H. & Spiegel, D. (1978). *Trance and treatment: Clinical uses of hypnosis.* New York: Basic Books.

Spindler, G. D. (1980). *The making of psychological anthropology.* Berkeley: University of California Press.

Spradley, J. (Ed.). (1972). *Culture and cognition.* San Francisco: Chandler.

Steers, R. D. & Porter, L. W. (Eds.) (1979). *Motivation and work behavior* (2nd ed.). New York: McGraw-Hill.

Sternbach, R. A. (1966). *Principles of psychophysiology.* New York: Academic Press.

Straus, G. (1976). Organization development. In R. Dubin (Ed.), *Handbook of work, organization and society.* New York: Free Press.

Sundberg, N. D. (1977). *Assessment of persons.* Englewood Cliffs, NJ: Prentice-Hall.

Super, D. E. & Crites, J. O. (1962). *Appraising vocational fitness.* New York: Harper & Row.

Sze, W. C. (1975). *The human life cycle.* New York: Jason Aronson.

Tannenbaum, R. & Davis, S. A. (1969). Values of man and organizations. *Industrial Management Review, 10* (2), 67–86.

Taylor, S. E. & Brown, J. D. (1988). Illusion and well-being: A social psychological perspective on mental health. *Psychological Bulletin 103,* 193–210.

Terborg, J. R. (1976). Motivation, behavior, and performance: A closer examination of goal setting and monetary incentives. *Journal of Applied Psychology, 61,* 613–621.

Thompson, J. D. (1967). *Organizations in action.* New York: McGraw-Hill.

Tolbert, E. L. (1980). *Counseling for career development* (2nd ed.). Boston: Houghton Mifflin.

Triandis, H. C. (1972). *The analysis of subjective culture.* New York: John Wiley.

Ullmann L. P., Krasner, L. (1966). *Case studies in behavior modification* (pp. 1–63). New York: Holt, Rinehart & Winston.

Vaillant, G. E. (1977). *Adaptation to life.* Boston: Little, Brown.

Van Maanen, J. & Kunda, G. (1986). Real feelings: Emotional expression and organizational culture. In B. Staw & L. L. Cummings (Eds.), *Research in organizational behavior.* Greenwich, CT: JAI Press.

Vondracek, F. W., Lerner, R. M., & Schulenberg, J. E. (In press). *Career development: A life span developmental approach.* Hillsdale, NJ: Lawrence Erlbaum.

Vroom, V. H. (1964). *Work and motivation.* New York: John Wiley.

Walker, J. W. & Gutteridge, T. G. (1979). *Career planning practices.* New York: AMACOM.

Watzlawick, P., Weakland, J., & Fisch, R. (1974). *Change: Principles of problem formation and problem resolution.* New York: Norton.

Webb, S. G. (1982). *Marketing and strategic planning for professional service firms.* New York: AMACOM.

Weick, K. (1979). *The social psychology of organizing* (2nd ed.). Reading, MA: Addison-Wesley.

Weinberg, G. M. (1985). *The secrets of consulting: A guide to giving & getting advice successfully.* New York: Dorset House.

Weiner, H. (1977). *Psychobiology and human disease.* New York: American Elsevier.

Weisbord, M. R. (1978). *Organizational diagnosis.* Reading, MA: Addison-Wesley.

Weiss, S. M., Herd, J. A., & Fox, B. H. (Eds.). (1981). *Perspectives on behavioral medicine.* New York: Academic Press.

Wells, L. E. & Marwell, G. (1976). *Self-esteem: Its conceptualization and measurement.* Beverly Hills, CA: Sage.

Wheatley, E. W. (1983). *Marketing professional services.* Englewood Cliffs, NJ: Prentice Hall.

White, R. W. (1959). Motivation reconsidered: The concept of competence. *Psychological Review, 66,* 297–333.

White, R. W. (1960). Competence and psychological stages. *Nebraska Symposium on Motivation.* Lincoln, NE: University of Nebraska Press.

Whiteley, J. M. & Resnikoff, A. (Eds.). (1978). *Career counseling.* Monterey, CA: Brooks/Cole.

Wiggins, J. S. (1973). *Personality and prediction: Principles of personality assessment.* Reading, MA: Addison-Wesley.

Wilson, A. (1972). *The marketing of professional services.* London: McGraw-Hill.

Wyer, R. S. & Scrull, T. K. (Eds.) (1984). *Handbook of social cognition.* Hillsdale, NJ: Erlbaum.

Wylie, R. C. (1979). *The self-concept: Theory and research on selected topics.* Lincoln, NE: University of Nebraska Press.

Yeager, J. (1983). A model for executive performance coaching. In J. S. J. Manuso (Ed.), *Occupational clinical psychology.* New York: Praeger.

Zeig, J. K. (1980). *A teaching seminar with Milton H. Erickson.* New York: Brunner/Mazel.

Zeig, J. K. (Ed.). (1988). *The evolution of psychotherapy.* New York: Brunner/Mazel.

Subject Index

181

Name Index

Adrian, C., 46
Aesop, 105
Agarwala-Rogers, R., 43
Allport, G. W., 7, 36
Anastasi, A., 30
Anderson, A. R., 36
Appley, M. H., 30
Arbiter, P., 56
Argyris, C., 7
Assante, M. K., 43
Atkinson, J. W., 30

Bakal, D. A., 36
Baltes, P. B., 36
Bandura, A., 46
Barber, J., 46
Barker, P. A., 44
Bass, B. M., 7
Baum, A., 36
Bazerman, M. H., 11
Beck, A. T., 46
Beckhard, R., 7
Beier, E. G., 55
Bell, C. H., 7
Bellows, R., 7, 44
Bennis, W., 7
Berger, J., 104
Blake, R. R., 7, 43
Bloom, P., 110
Bond, L., 36
Bonica, J. J., 46
Bowen, D. D., 36
Bradley, L. A., 36
Brady, J. P., 36
Bray, D. M., 7, 36
Bridges, W. E., 36

Brim, O. G., 36
Bronowski, J., 26, 36
Brooks, L., 7
Brown, D., 7
Bryne, D., 43
Buckholdt, D. R., 36
Buckley, W., 7
Bugental, J. F. T., 46, 48
Burke, W. W., 7
Butcher, J. N., 30

Campbell, K. J., 7
Campbell, J. P., 7
Caplan, R., 7
Chesney, M. A., 36
Chiriboga, 36
Clionsky, M. I., 44
Cofer, C. N., 36
Cogger, J. C., 30
Cohen, B. P., 104
Cole, M., 43
Collison, D. R., 46
Connor, R. A., 110
Cooper, C. L., 7, 46
Cramer, S. H., 36
Crasilneck, H. B., 46

Dagenais, J. F., 97
Daniel, N., 43
Datan, N., 36
Davidson, J. P.
Davis, S. A., 36
Davison, G. C., 46
Deci, E. L., 9
Dennerstein, L., 46
Dickinson, E., 1

185